UP IN ARMS

A
Common Cause
Guide To
Understanding
Nuclear Arms
Policy

S A N D R A   S E D A C C A

Dedicated to the memory of
Ellis Williams,
Common Cause Volunteer
1976–1983

UP IN ARMS

A Common Cause Guide To Understanding Nuclear Arms Policy

SANDRA SEDACCA

Dedicated to the memory of
Ellis Williams,
Common Cause Volunteer
1976–1983

I like to believe that people, in the long run, are going to do more to promote peace than our governments. Indeed, I think that people want peace so much that one of these days governments had better get out of their way and let them have it.

President Dwight D. Eisenhower
1959

ACKNOWLEDGMENTS

This guide to nuclear arms policy reflects the efforts of many staff members, interns, and volunteers at Common Cause. Patient guidance and supervision came from Stephen Hitchner, Jr., Vice President for Issue Development, and D. Michal Freedman, Associate Director for Issue Development. Lynn Rusten offered valuable assistance throughout the project, producing initial drafts of several chapters and editing subsequent versions. Special thanks go to Stephen Seitz and Ed Cox for their careful editorial and administrative support and to Kathy Walsh for managing production of this guide. Individuals who contributed research and writing included Katherine Elwood, Helene Epstein, Robert Hill, Karen Pollitz, Eric Sanders, Stephen Seitz, Tom Street and Ellis Williams.

Up In Arms is a staff endeavor and does not necessarily represent the views of individual members of the Governing Board of Common Cause. Although Common Cause takes full responsibility for the final product, several individuals deserve mention for their helpful comments on an earlier draft of the manuscript: the staff of the Arms Control Association, Anne Cahn, John Cavanaugh, Dick Clark, Elise Garcia, Florence Graves, Jay Hedlund, Admiral Gene LaRocque, Ann McBride, Stan Norris, Jeremy Rosner, Penny Wakefield and Lawrence Weiler. Finally, a personal note of appreciation to my husband, Sherwood Ives, who also helped make this book possible.

Sandra Sedacca
Senior Research Associate

TABLE OF CONTENTS

FOREWORD

"One man can make a difference and every man should try." On the philosophy so expressed by President John F. Kennedy, Common Cause was founded over a decade ago: Individual citizens can and should control the affairs of government.

The book you now hold in your hands, *Up In Arms*, seeks to give the average citizen the information—the terminology, the strategies and tactics, the competing arguments, and more—required to participate effectively in the nuclear arms debate. And citizens must be involved. The so-called nuclear priesthood all too easily forgets that the strategies and tactics it debates will affect not faceless numbers but millions of individual husbands, wives, children, and friends, and also the generations that might follow. A measure of expertise is essential to understanding the facts, but common sense also is necessary to wisdom, and wisdom is essential to determine what must be done. As citizens, we must make our common sense and wisdom felt, or risk losing all.

The nuclear arms issue is the paramount issue of our times. I urge you to become involved either by joining organizations such as Common Cause, or by writing to government officials, or by any other means that appeals to you. But above all else, I urge you to care enough *to do something*. Citizens can make a difference and every citizen should try.

Archibald Cox
Chairman, Common Cause

INTRODUCTION

Twenty years ago, Senator Everett Dirksen spoke of the threat of nuclear war in a speech before the United States Senate. "One of my age thinks about his destiny a little," he said. "I should not like to have written on my tombstone, 'He knew what happened at Hiroshima, but he did not take a first step.'"

Today individuals across the nation and around the world are taking their first steps to help prevent nuclear war. Public complacency has given way to genuine concern about the dangers of nuclear weapons. Indifference has been transformed into attentiveness as nuclear arms control has moved to the top of the public's agenda.

Why are citizens up in arms about the threat of nuclear war? In the past, the public has looked to politicians and technicians, to diplomats and generals, for answers to the nuclear dilemma. Today, citizens also are looking to each other—their instincts and intuition as well as their intelligence—for guidance.

First, citizens instinctively sense that the arms race poses a very real threat to their survival. Alarmed by the prospect of nuclear holocaust, they fear for their families, their friends, and their futures. They understand the stakes and find the risks plainly unacceptable.

Second, citizens intuitively question the logic of the nuclear arms race. Confounded by experts who offer conflicting theories, they recognize the need for fresh, common sense approaches to the problem of nuclear rivalry. They have heard too much doubletalk and are unconvinced.

Finally, citizens appreciate the power of knowledge and information. Baffled by the jargon of nuclear weaponry—megatonnage, kill ratios, throw-weight, and the like—they realize the value of doing their homework. They admit to the complexity of the nuclear issue but want to be better informed.

That is where we begin this guide—with doing our homework. Learning the basic facts. Mastering the concepts. Studying the alternatives. It is a slow process of self-education, but one that is worthwhile. It will help us think about the nuclear issue as concerned citizens. It will help us ask tough questions of those officials responsible for our national security. Finally, it will help us recognize sound government policies when we see them—policies that reduce the nuclear peril and move us toward a more certain peace.

In preparing this guide, Common Cause has sought to identify the questions that are basic to understanding the threat of nuclear war and ways of reducing that threat. By examining these questions in a systematic manner, we hope to help citizens develop a framework for making judgments about nuclear arms issues, judgments in which they can have confidence.

In Part One, we begin our inquiry by considering the basis for current fears about nuclear war. How grave is the threat of nuclear war?

In Part Two, we survey the nuclear arsenals of the superpowers in relation to each other. How do U.S. and Soviet nuclear forces compare?

In Part Three, we examine different ways the nuclear threat can be minimized through public policy. How can nuclear war be prevented?

In Part Four, we address the special concerns that arise from negotiating arms control agreements with the Soviet Union, our primary nuclear rival. How should we deal with the Soviet Union?

Finally, we conclude our inquiry by exploring the unique role of citizens in the nuclear arms debate. How can citizens influence nuclear arms policy?

The central premise of this guide is the value of education. To participate in the current dialogue on nuclear arms policy, citizens must have the confidence and ability to examine the issues from all sides. To help move the dialogue in new directions, they must understand the ideas that have guided our nuclear policies in the past and shaped current thinking on nuclear arms control.

Ultimately, the process of education is a process of empowerment: creating the opportunity for citizens to have an effective voice in the debate on preventing nuclear war. By participating directly in the political process—through voting, lobbying, and other tools of democracy—citizens can influence the direction of nuclear arms policy in the future. In the words of Common Cause Chairman Archibald Cox:

A free governing people cannot afford to leave the formulation of nuclear arms policy to so-called "experts." Too often the experts become trapped and blinded by their special roles: the military by the duty to plan for war; the scientists and technicians engaged in weapons development by enthusiasm to build and test the products of their imagination and hours of effort; industries by the lure of government contracts. Peace and threats to peace are the people's business.

This citizen's guide has been prepared in that spirit and in the hope that each of us, empowered with knowledge about nuclear war, will be better equipped as advocates of peace.

I. HOW GRAVE IS THE THREAT OF NUCLEAR WAR?

Never in my 35 years of public service have I been so afraid of nuclear war.

George Kennan
Former U.S. Ambassador to
the Soviet Union
1981

What Would Happen in a Nuclear War?

Concern about nuclear war can be traced to a basic human interest in survival. Nuclear weapons have brought with them the terrifying possibility that a war would end life on earth as we know it. Citizens and policymakers alike approach this frightening subject hoping to reconcile a desire for security with the perils of the nuclear age. Columnist Ellen Goodman describes this dilemma in her article "Making Our Lives Under the Bomb":

> How do we live with this bomb? Do we live as if the end were inevitable, and opt for the private pleasures of life? Do we live as if change were possible? Do we live as if we can plan for old age?

The answers to these questions depend, to a large extent, on one's perceptions of the nuclear threat. In this context, it is important for citizens to examine the danger of nuclear war and to consider its implications for personal, national, and even global security.

Ironically, the process of acquiring expertise about nuclear war sometimes results in a detachment from its human costs. Roger Molander, founder of Ground Zero and nuclear strategist for the National Security Council in the Carter Administration, relates his experience with this problem:

> I recall one Saturday a colleague came into the think tank office with his wife to find me sticking different-colored pins—representing different-sized weapons—into a map of the Soviet Union. . . . My colleague's wife was horrified. But when the pin went into Minsk or Moscow, I didn't see people working or children playing. . . . I just stuck in the pins.

In joining the debate over nuclear arms policy, informed citizens can bring to bear an appreciation of the life and death issues at stake as well as the political and military choices that must be faced. To grasp the consequences of nuclear war, it is appropriate to begin by reflecting upon humanity's past experience with nuclear weapons.

■ Past Victims

At 8:15 a.m. on August 6, 1945, the United States dropped the first atomic bomb on the Japanese city of Hiroshima. The bomb killed more than 66,000 people almost immediately and injured nearly 100,000 others. The entire city was left in ruins, with roughly 80 percent of its buildings destroyed or damaged. Three days later, a second bomb was dropped on Nagasaki, causing 40,000 immediate deaths and destroying 40 percent of the city's structures.

Since the close of World War II, historians, physicians, psychiatrists, and sociologists have documented the outcome of the Japanese bombings in great detail. Some of the most telling information, however, comes from younger "experts": Japanese school children who recorded their own experiences of the A-bomb in school compositions. The words of Shigeko Hirata, written while a sixth-grader in Hiroshima, capture their suffering:

I was five when I was caught in the atom bomb.

After seeing Father off to the office I was playing in front of the house.

Suddenly there was a burst of yellow smoke and an indescribably loud noise. I seemed to hear from a distance my mother's voice calling, "Grandma! Shige!"

I felt as though something were pressing on me and I couldn't move. Gradually the smoke thinned and I could make out what had happened to the house. Mother finally managed to make her way out of the smashed kitchen. Inside the house there was no place to step for the mess of broken window glass, wall plaster and tangled floor matting. Grandma was ill and had been lying in the bedroom and she was blown as she was, all wrapped up in bedding, into the next room and the floor matting was on top of her. Fortunately she wasn't injured at all.

"Help! Help!"

Hearing this call, Mother rushed next door and found the neighbor's grandmother caught under the ruins of the house. Mother picked off the roof tiles, timbers and glass one at a time and got her out. Flames rose nearby. We couldn't stay another minute. Mother took Grandmother on her back and climbed up the river bank.

People came fleeing from the nearby streets. One after another they were almost unrecognizable. The skin was burned off some of them and was hanging from their hands and from their chins; their faces were red and so swollen that you could hardly tell where their eyes and mouths were. From the houses smoke black enough to scorch the heavens was covering the sky. It was a horrible sight. I clung to Mother trembling all over. At that point Father came running up with an indescribable expression on his face. He had a dreadful wound on his back and you could not say whether it was black or yellow but it was a terrible color. The hair on his head looked as though it were covered with ashes.

As we were fleeing along the road we passed gradually more and more people who hadn't the strength to go farther and had fallen there. To this very day if I close my eyes I remember all those sights that I saw then and I feel as if I were trembling again.

The Hiroshima and Nagasaki bombs produced explosions equivalent to 14 and 20 thousand tons of chemical high explosives, power described as 14 or 20 *kilotons (kt),* respectively. Today, there are some 50 thousand nuclear warheads in the world, with their explosive power ranging from about 100 tons up to more than 20 million tons, or 20 *megatons (mt),* of TNT. The combined strength of current nuclear arsenals represents an explosive force of some 13 thousand million tons of TNT—the equivalent of one million Hiroshima bombs or more than three tons of TNT for every man, woman, and child on earth.

■ Future Victims?

It is difficult to fathom the staggering size of today's nuclear stockpile and its vast potential for destruction. The prospect of actually unleashing such power defies the imagination of policymakers and citizens alike.

At the request of the Senate Committee on Foreign Relations, the Office of Technology Assessment (OTA), an arm of the U.S. Congress, initiated a study in 1979 to "put what have been abstract measures of strategic power into more comprehensive terms." The product of this inquiry is a 150-page report, entitled *The Effects of Nuclear War,* describing the possible consequences of nuclear war for the civilian populations, economies, and societies of the United States and the Soviet Union. Its powerful findings are summarized below.*

The Effects of Nuclear Weapons

Unlike other questions about nuclear war, there is a substantial consensus regarding the general effects of nuclear explosions. Most experts agree on what nuclear weapons would do to people and structures in urban areas.

Blast

Most damage to cities from nuclear weapons comes from the explosive blast. The blast drives air away from the site of

---

*New calculations announced at a 1983 conference of scientists suggest that prior findings, such as those of OTA, may understate the effects of nuclear war. This subject is discussed under the heading "The Role of Uncertainty."

the explosion, producing sudden changes in air pressure—called *overpressure*—that can crush objects, as well as high winds that can move them suddenly and knock them down. In general, large buildings are destroyed by overpressure, while people and objects such as trees and utility poles are destroyed by the wind. Most blast deaths result from the collapse of occupied buildings, from people being blown into objects, or from objects—such as flying glass—being blown into people.

Heat and Light

Heat from a nuclear weapon's explosion—known as *thermal radiation*—can cause severe burn injuries to people, depending on their proximity to "ground zero," the point of detonation. A one-megaton explosion can inflict first degree burns at distances of about seven miles, second degree burns at six miles, and third degree burns, the most severe, at five miles—causing shock and death in the absence of adequate medical care. People closer to ground zero would be incinerated by the heat. Thermal radiation also can ignite kindling materials directly, causing individual and mass fires that endanger populations and property. The visible light from an explosion can produce temporary "flashblindness" in people who are looking in its direction; permanent retinal damage also may occur.

Radiation

Nuclear weapons inflict ionizing radiation on people in two different ways. *Direct radiation* occurs at the time of the explosion; it can be very intense, but its range is limited. *Fallout radiation* refers to particles made radioactive by the effects of the explosion and subsequently distributed at varying distances from the site of the blast. In the short term, people exposed to high levels of radiation will die, and those exposed to lesser amounts may become acutely ill from vomiting and fever. In the long term, cancer, other illnesses, genetic damage and death may result.

Electrical and Magnetic Energy

A nuclear weapons explosion produces an *electromagnetic pulse (EMP)*, a phenomenon likened to electric fields from radio waves or lightning. This instantaneous and enormous burst of energy, measured in volts per meter, can cause severe damage to a city's electrical or electronic systems, such as power lines and antennas. There is no evidence that EMP is a direct physical threat to humans; however, resulting communications and power shortages can hamper rescue operations and medical treatment.

These general descriptions explain how nuclear explosions cause injury and death to people, as well as damage and destruction to property. To understand the aggregate implications of nuclear weapons effects, it is important to consider the scope of civilian damage that would occur as the result of a nuclear attack.

The Scope of Civilian Damage

There are any number of types of attacks that could occur in a nuclear conflict, including attacks on urban populations, attacks on the industrial base, and attacks on military forces. To predict the scope of civilian damage, the Office of Technology Assessment distinguishes among the different "attack cases."

Attack on a Single City

Suppose a nuclear attack were launched against Detroit or Leningrad, cities with estimated populations of 4.3 million each. Depending on the details of the attack, the immediate death toll could range from 200,000 to 2 million people. As many as 400,000 to 1 million injuries could occur, ultimately resulting in many more fatalities. Under the worst conditions, all habitable housing, hospitals, and heavy industry would be destroyed. In this case, rescue and recovery operations—including food, water, medical, and sanitation supplies—would have to be supported totally from outside the area. Even with such assistance, however, medical facilities would be inadequate to care for the injured. For example, the entire United States has facilities to treat 1,000 or 2,000 severe burn cases; a single nuclear weapon could produce more than 10,000.

Attack on the Industrial Base

Suppose a nuclear attack were launched against oil refineries in the United States or the Soviet Union. The immediate fatalities could range from 1 million Soviet deaths to 5 million U.S. deaths, given the proximity of refineries to residential areas and the size of the weapons used. Hundreds of thousands of additional fatalities could result from injuries and cancer. Such a Soviet attack would destroy 64 percent of American oil refining capacity, while a U.S. attack would destroy 73 percent of the more-concentrated Soviet refining capacity—again depending on the details of the attack. The disappearance of fuel would cause severe industrial decline and social disruption, creating particular hardships for Soviet agriculture and for the petroleum-dependent American economy.

Attack on Nuclear Forces

Suppose an attack were launched against American or Soviet nuclear forces, including missile silos, bomber airfields,

The Role of Uncertainty

Predicting the outcome of nuclear war is not an exact science. In an actual nuclear attack, the extent of death and destruction would be affected by a number of variables, including the number, location, and size of the bombs detonated, the height of their burst, the time of day and year of the attack, and the wind and weather conditions.

For example, the time of day would affect whether people were concentrated in factories and offices or dispersed in suburbs. The time of year, such as harvest time, could affect the degree of fallout damage to agriculture; wintertime could lead to greater fatalities from cold and exposure. Weather conditions, particularly the speed and direction of wind, would affect the extent and location of fallout contamination. The amount of moisture in the air would greatly influence the number and spread of fires.

Each of these variables, along with many others, compounds the problem of predicting the outcome of nuclear attack. Moreover, there are many effects of nuclear war that defy calculation.

How would individuals cope with massive housing, food, and water shortages? Would disease spread into major debilitating epidemics? Would all governmental organization disintegrate into anarchy? There is simply no reliable way to measure these consequences of nuclear war, yet they are "at least as important as those for which calculations are attempted," states the Office of Technology Assessment. Therefore, any estimates, however careful, should be viewed with caution: ". . . the nonmilitary observer should remember that actual damage is likely to be greater than that reflected in military calculations."

Indeed, scientific tools for calculating the effects of nuclear war are changing over time. For example, until recently scientists had not calculated in detail what would happen to the world's climate after a nuclear war. New evidence, based on computer models of the earth's weather system, suggests that the detonation of even 100 megatons on cities—a relatively small-scale attack—would produce a cloud of smoke and debris that could block sunlight, cause temperatures to plunge, and create a harsh "nuclear winter." An all-out nuclear exchange could so disrupt the earth's biological support systems that the extinction of much of the earth's plant and even animal life could occur. These projections reflect the consensus of many scientists gathered at the 1983 Conference on the Long-Term Worldwide Biological Consequences of Nuclear War. Their conclusions, however speculative, are likely to have profound implications for public understanding of the nuclear threat. As keynote speaker Donald Kennedy of Stanford University said:

. . . the history of our development of nuclear knowledge, as well as the complexity of many of the longer-range effects . . . suggest that uncertainty ought to be a thematic warning to the policy planners. What our most thoughtful projections show is that a major nuclear exchange will have, among its plausible effects, the greatest biological and physical disruptions of this planet in its last 65 million years . . . . That assessment of prospective risk needs to form a background for everyone who bears responsibility for national security decisions, here and elsewhere.●

Can Civil Defense Make a Difference?

Official estimates of civilian deaths in a nuclear war often are based on assumptions about civil defense. Two types of measures commonly are considered: protecting people in specially designed shelters, known as *sheltering,* and/or evacuating people from high-risk to low-risk areas, known as *crisis relocation.*

The debate about civil defense centers largely on the question of its effectiveness. Most observers concur that evacuation and sheltering theoretically could save lives, but many doubt whether such protection would be feasible in an actual nuclear war. In the aftermath of an attack, shelters in the vicinity of the explosion would heat to intolerable temperatures, burning and asphyxiating their inhabitants. Shelters in "safer" areas, even if stocked in advance, quickly would be depleted of food, water, medical, and sanitation supplies. In addition, large-scale evacuation to these safer areas would demand extraordinary coordination during a time of panic, placing an impossible burden on road and transportation systems. Moreover, such "host" communities also could be targeted by enemy missiles, thus eliminating their protective function. Given these problems, the Office of Technology Assessment notes, "The effectiveness of civil defense measures depends, among other things, on the events

and submarine bases. This type of attack, known as a *counterforce attack,* would produce more than 1 million fatalities in the United States or the Soviet Union. Under worst conditions, American deaths could reach 20 million and Soviet deaths, more than 10 million, depending on the spread of fallout to populated areas. Long-term cancer deaths and genetic damage could affect millions as well. Such massive fatalities would cause enormous economic disruption and disorganization in both nations; the U.S. marketplace, in particular, would experience abrupt shifts in demand and supply. The long-term process of recovery also would be complicated by extreme psychological suffering among survivors as a result of the staggering loss of life.

Full-scale Attack

Suppose an all-out attack were launched against urban, industrial, and military centers in the United States or the Soviet Union. American deaths could range from 35 to 77 percent of the population (from 70 million to 160 million dead) and Soviet deaths, from 20 percent to 40 percent of the population (50 million to 100 million dead), given certain assumptions about attack conditions.

Additional millions of people subsequently would die from injuries, disease, starvation, and, ultimately, radiation effects. The survivors would find themselves in a "race for survival." Their prospects would turn on innumerable factors: the extent of actual physical damage; the availability of resources to support surviving populations and economic recovery; the possibility of social and psychological disruption and collapse. Under the worst conditions, concludes OTA, ". . . the future of civilization itself in the nations attacked would be in doubt."

These stark projections of civilian damage relate the aggregate destruction that would occur during a nuclear attack on the United States or the Soviet Union. But what would it be *like?* In an effort to capture the immediate horror of an actual attack, Drs. David Barash and Judith Lipton describe the effects of a single one-megaton bomb, having the explosive power of 70 Hiroshima bombs, detonated in one city:*

The bomb explodes with the heat of the sun and the stars, and within the first 2 seconds, the center of the

---

*Although many projections typically describe the effects of a one-megaton bomb, it is probable that an actual attack would involve many multimegaton weapons aimed at major targets. Moreover, most analyses do not contemplate the effect of repeated attacks in the hours, days, or weeks following an initial explosion.

city, including steel and concrete buildings, asphalt, roads, bridges, brick, glass, people, plants, and animals are vaporized. If a groundburst, the center of the city is turned into a crater, 1,000 feet in diameter and 200 feet deep, surrounded by a rim of highly radioactive debris of about twice this diameter.

Within the first 2 seconds after the detonation, the fireball grows rapidly, emitting gamma rays and neutrons, as well as infrared radiation, pulsing outward at the speed of light. The blinding flash melts the eyeballs of anyone looking on from close to the explosion, and causes retinal burns to anyone who reflexively glances at it from within 50 miles. Within a radius of 1.75 miles, steel surfaces evaporate, concrete surfaces explode, glass melts, and people are melted and then charred. At 2.75 miles, aluminum siding evaporates, auto sheet metal and lucite windows melt. (People fare no better.) At 4.35 miles, wood, plastics, and heavy fabrics burst into flames, and asphalt surfaces melt. At 5.5 miles from the detonation, upholstery, canvas, and clothing burst into flames, and painted surfaces explode. Watching the destruction of a city with a nuclear bomb, one would first see it melt, char, then collapse. Whatever is left would then likely roar into flames. An individual human being, say two miles from ground zero, within the first 2 seconds would receive fatal total body irradiation, plus third degree burns. Her clothing would catch fire, along with her skin, and she would quickly be reduced to a charred corpse.

Such words are a grim reminder of the perils posed by nuclear weaponry. There is little doubt that any nuclear attack—whatever the actual wartime conditions—would cause vast devastation and suffering. The effects of even one of the smaller long-range weapons currently in Soviet and American arsenals would be far greater than those of any bomb ever exploded on a populated region of the earth.

The human stakes in preventing nuclear war thus are enormously high, dwarfing all other issues of national security. We rely on nuclear weapons to protect our nation, but they also have the potential to destroy it. In facing this dilemma, we can look to historical experience and technical expertise for some solutions, but human judgment and imagination must furnish the rest.

leading up to the attack, the enemy's targeting policy, and sheer luck."

Despite such uncertainties, some government officials have expressed confidence in crisis relocation as a means of limiting casualties in a nuclear war. Yet many observers—particularly in the medical community—challenge this view as unrealistic. Dr. Howard Hiatt, Dean of the Harvard School of Public Health, told a Senate committee in June 1980:

Recent talk by public figures about winning or even surviving a nuclear war must reflect a widespread failure to appreciate a medical reality: any nuclear war would inevitably cause death, disease and suffering of epidemic proportions and effective medical interventions on any realistic scale would be impossible.

■ Selected Sources

Ruth Adams and Susan Cullen, eds., *The Final Epidemic: Physicians and Scientists on Nuclear War* (Educational Foundation for Nuclear Science, Inc., 1981).

David P. Barash and Judith Eve Lipton, *Stop Nuclear War! A Handbook* (Grove Press, Inc., 1982).

Ellen Goodman, "Making Our Lives Under the Bomb," *The Washington Post,* August 10, 1982.

Constance Holden, "Scientists Describe 'Nuclear Winter'," *Science,* November 18, 1983 (reprints of technical papers presented at the Conference on the Long-Term Worldwide Biological Consequences of Nuclear War are published in *Science,* December 23, 1983).

Roger Molander, "How I Learned to Start Worrying and Hate the Bomb," *The Washington Post,* March 21, 1982.

Arada Osada, ed., *Children of the A-Bomb* (Midwest Publishers, International, 1982).

Jonathan Schell, *The Fate of The Earth* (Alfred A. Knopf, 1982).

U.S. Congress, Office of Technology Assessment, *The Effects of Nuclear War* (Government Printing Office, May 1979).

Thinking about nuclear war evokes a discordant sense of urgency yet complacency in many observers. The effects of nuclear weapons are so grim and far-reaching that the prospect of their use seems comfortably far-fetched. British defense scholar Lawrence Freedman describes this quandary in his book *The Evolution of Nuclear Strategy*:

> The essence of the problem is the difficulty of attaching any rationality whatsoever to the initiation of a chain of events that could well end in the utter devastation of one's own society.

The very fact that nuclear weapons exist demands that serious attention be given to their possible use. To avoid a nuclear war—and to improve, as a nation, our tools for crisis management and crisis prevention—we need to understand how nuclear war might start.

■ Possible Nuclear Triggers

The term *scenario* frequently is used to describe the chain of events that could lead to nuclear confrontation between the United States and the Soviet Union. The most commonly recognized scenarios tend to fall under three broad groupings: bolt from the blue, conflict escalation, and isolated incidents.

Bolt from the Blue

The prospect of sudden nuclear attack has received widespread attention in military circles as well as in public debate. Known as a *bolt from the blue,* this scenario describes an unexpected nuclear strike by the Soviet Union on the United States, or vice versa, during a period of seemingly normal relations.

Preoccupation with nuclear surprise is understandable, given its frightening implications. According to Richard Betts of the Brookings Institution, "Military surprise is among the greatest dangers a country can face. Of the major wars in Europe, Asia, and the Middle East that have reshaped the international balance of power over the past several decades, most began with sudden attacks." Preparations for a bolt from the blue are an integral part of U.S. military planning:

What is a Strategic Nuclear Strike?

Although the phrase "strategic nuclear strike" commonly is used by defense specialists, its literal meaning is not well-known to much of the public. In American military planning, **strategic nuclear weapons** refers to a certain part of the U.S. nuclear arsenal—long-range nuclear forces that go from our country, or our submarines at sea, to the Soviet Union. These are distinguished from **theater nuclear weapons**—intermediate-range forces designed for use in a given area of operations (e.g., the European theater)—and from **tactical nuclear weapons**—short-range nuclear forces designed for combat use on the battlefield. (Weapons that are not nuclear in nature—guns, tanks, and the like—are called conventional military forces.) A strategic nuclear strike, then, refers to a nuclear attack in which long-range nuclear weapons are launched directly against the territory of the United States or the Soviet Union. •

U.S. nuclear forces are kept at day-to-day alert levels and are judged for their overall adequacy in relation to conditions of sudden attack.

Nevertheless, such a scenario is regarded by most defense and arms control experts as the *least* likely path to nuclear war. As Walter Slocombe, Deputy Under Secretary of Defense for Policy Planning in the Carter Administration, writes:

> It is highly unlikely that the Soviets would attack the United States (and still more implausible that the United States would attack the Soviet Union) as a deliberate calculated act divorced from an immediate and intense political and probably military confrontation.

In a similar vein, Desmond Ball of the International Institute of Strategic Studies says:

> . . . a strategic nuclear strike by the United States or the Soviet Union against targets in the other's heartland—no matter how limited, precise, or controlled it might be—is most unlikely to be the first move in any conflict between them.

The prospect of nuclear surprise is considered remote for several reasons. To be successful, a surprise attack would have to be perfect, disarming and paralyzing the enemy's nuclear forces. Given the technical uncertainties of a large-scale attack, the likelihood of advance warning, and the tremendous risk of nuclear retaliation, no rational leader could take such a step with confidence.

Although a bolt from the blue cannot be discounted completely, its implausibility thus is well-recognized. Unfortunately, government officials often place disproportionate emphasis on this scenario in their public policy statements—an approach that distorts the nature of the nuclear risk and impedes public understanding of national defense needs.

Conflict Escalation

Unlike a bolt from the blue, the *conflict escalation* scenario contemplates nuclear confrontation between the United States and the Soviet Union during a period of heightened hostility and military conflict. Marshall Shulman, Director of the Russian Institute at Columbia University and formerly a government advisor on Soviet affairs, explains the sequence of events as follows:

> The concern that seems most to be watched for is the risk of escalation from a local conflict, and particularly if the separation between nuclear and conventional weapons becomes blurred. If there is an initial conflict and both sides get involved because their interests are involved, there are neither technical nor political checkpoints in the passage from a conventional military

engagement up through battlefield nuclears.

It is widely recognized that *any* use of nuclear weapons during a crisis—by the United States, the Soviet Union, or a third party—would heighten the danger of escalation to full-scale nuclear war. Several geographic areas pose particular risks of military conflict between the superpowers.

Europe

The prospect of Soviet attack in Europe is a central issue in U.S. military planning. One scenario contemplates an uprising in East Germany that would draw into conflict troops from the Western alliance, organized under the North Atlantic Treaty Organization (NATO), and the Soviet-East European alliance, known as the Warsaw Pact. Either side, fearing military disadvantage, might resort to nuclear weapons to stop the enemy's advance.*

The likelihood of a Soviet invasion of Western Europe, although plausible, is open to debate. According to former U.S. officials McGeorge Bundy, George Kennan, Robert McNamara, and Gerard Smith:

> That risk has never been as great as prophets of doom have claimed and has always lain primarily in the possibility that Soviet leaders might think they could achieve some quick and limited gain that would be accepted because no defense or reply could be concerted. That temptation has been much reduced by the Allied conventional deployments achieved in the last 20 years . . . .

Nevertheless, most experts concur on the inescapable danger of escalation, should a military conflict in Europe occur. As Dean Rusk, Secretary of State under Presidents Kennedy and Johnson, observes:

> Anyone who thinks that an all-out Soviet attack on Western Europe, including the American conventional and nuclear forces stationed there, would not lead to an all-out nuclear war is living in a dream world.

The Middle East

Conflict escalation in the Persian Gulf area is most likely to result, says Brookings scholar Richard Betts, from three conditions: the persistence of the Arab-Israeli conflict, in which the superpowers are engaged as patrons of the contending parties; the dependence of the Western industrialized states on supplies of petroleum from the region; and the actual or potential political instability of all the Persian Gulf states.

Any outbreak of armed hostilities involving such key inter-

---

*In fact, it has long been U.S. and NATO policy that, in the event of a conventional conflict in Europe, the United States would, if deemed necessary, initiate the use of nuclear weapons, with the threat of escalation up the "nuclear ladder" to an all-out strategic exchange. This issue is discussed in Chapter 3 under the heading "Deterring War in Europe."

ests as Israel, Saudi Arabia, or Iran could result in a U.S.-Soviet conventional conflict that escalates to nuclear war. In addition, the acquisition of nuclear weapons by neighboring states could increase the volatility of the region. Many experts believe that Israel already has or is close to having nuclear weapons; by the year 2000, Egypt, Saudi Arabia, and Iraq are expected to have comparable capability. Any use of nuclear weapons by these nations could provoke a "catalytic war" that draws the superpowers into conflict or could trigger a regional nuclear war that spreads to a global scale.

These grim scenarios are not confined to the Middle East: they could occur in any number of Third World "hot spots." Southern Africa, the Caribbean Basin, and the Korean Peninsula, among others, are rife with tension and ripe for superpower confrontation. Again, the spread of nuclear arms to these regions would increase the danger of nuclear war. Moreover, a recent U.S. intelligence survey, discussed in a *New York Times* report on November 15, 1982, estimates that 31 countries—many of them engaged in long-standing regional disputes—will be able to produce nuclear weapons by the year 2000.

Isolated Incidents

Typically, public debate on the nuclear threat focuses on "intentional" confrontation between the United States and the Soviet Union arising from deliberate and calculated military acts. Several alternative scenarios, often overlooked, envision random and isolated incidents that could precipitate the use of nuclear weapons.

The United States maintains an elaborate system for the *command and control* of nuclear forces—a network of personnel, procedures, and facilities designed to manage nuclear weapons operations in peacetime and in the event of national emergency. Despite the numerous checks and balances that characterize this system, its vulnerability to technical malfunction and human error is well-documented.

Accidents

All nuclear weapons operations, while varying from system to system, rely on intricate safety devices to guard against nuclear weapons accidents. These include sensors that respond to environmental changes and prevent inadvertent detonations.

Despite these precautions, many observers point with some concern to the record of "broken arrows"—nuclear weapons accidents—that have occurred over the years. The Department of Defense reports 32 accidents involving nuclear weapons in fires, aircraft collisions, and other emergencies from 1950 to 1980. Although all of these incidents involved severe stress, only two led to the dispersal of radioactive material, none resulted in a nuclear detonation, and none came even remotely close to triggering a nuclear conflict. Nevertheless, the risk of future nuclear weapons accidents must be taken seriously by the United States as well as other nuclear nations where safeguard systems may be less secure.

False Alarms

The United States currently relies on sophisticated warning technology to monitor missile tests, launches, flights, and attacks by Soviet nuclear forces. During the 1950s and 1960s, unrefined detection systems were susceptible to error and recorded, for example, natural phenomena such as a flight of geese or lunar reflection as missile warnings. Today's systems, although much improved, are still vulnerable to malfunction and even misuse. In November 1979, for example, a wargame practice tape was mistakenly played on a back-up computer of the North American Air Defense Command (NORAD); this human error triggered a nuclear attack warning that lasted six minutes until the error was discovered. On June 3 and 6, 1980, the mechanical failure of a computer chip caused computer circuits to generate and display false missile alert information.

The recurrence of such incidents—147 between January 1979 and June 1980, according to a report of the Senate Armed Services Committee—heightens concern that an undetected false signal could prompt a nuclear response by American leaders and escalate to war. Moreover, the risk of error is believed to be greater in the Soviet Union and other countries where warning technologies may be less sophisticated.

Unauthorized Use and Terrorism

At the highest levels of U.S. government, a system of sealed and coded "authenticator" cards is maintained so that the ultimate authorization for firing nuclear weapons comes from the President. At lower levels, electronic locks known as *permissive action links* are used to prevent the arming and release of weapons until special go-codes are fed into the mechanisms. The redundant combination of codes and keys and a nuclear "buddy system"—whereby no single person can fire a nuclear weapon—helps protect against unauthorized launches by an aberrant member of the military or by a terrorist.

Nevertheless, the prospect of nuclear terrorism poses a growing concern for defense planners. Increasing quantities of fissionable materials and nuclear weapons are being stored, transported, and dispersed, making them more susceptible to theft. In addition, technical refinements in the size and efficiency of nuclear weapons make them portable as "suitcase bombs," available for smuggling. These developments coincide with an alarming pattern of terrorist activity around the world. For example, a *New York Times* report on October 23, 1982, stated that the Red Brigades terrorists who kidnapped Brigadier General James Dozier in Italy in 1981 had been seeking information on U.S. nuclear storage sites in Europe.

Isolated acts of "nuclear violence" not only would cause immediate destruction, but could, in the confusion and horror surrounding such an event, precipitate a larger crisis involving nuclear retaliation. The rising threat of terrorism has prompted the U.S. Defense Nuclear Agency (DNA), a part of the Defense Department, to shift the emphasis of its security program and accelerate efforts to safeguard nuclear storage sites in the United States, Europe, and South Korea. "[T]he thing we worry most about today," says Colonel Charles Linton of DNA, "is the threat from a dedicated terrorist force."

Although the record of isolated nuclear incidents is sobering, there has never been a full Soviet-American alert of nuclear forces, despite technical and human failures in the warning and control system. Paul Bracken, author of *The Command and Control of Nuclear Forces,* explains why the system's complexity helps reduce the risk of accidental nuclear war:

> Discrete accidents are easy to design against. With so many checks and balances, procedures for authentication of orders, and independent human interventions overlaid onto the control system for strategic weapons, the likelihood of accidental or inadvertant war is very, very low in peacetime.

Moreover, in peacetime, non-alert conditions, U.S. and Soviet personnel can evaluate isolated incidents in the broader context of routine force deployments. They can take precautions and countermeasures without driving the system to a full alert. But, cautions Bracken, our complex command structure may respond differently during periods of political tension and heightened military activity when simultaneous but random events may compound the danger of war:

> . . . the overall effect of both Soviet and American actions might be to aggravate the crisis, forcing alert levels to rachet upward worldwide. Although each side might well believe it was taking necessary precautionary moves, the other side might see a precaution as a threat. This would in turn click the alert level upward another notch.

The plausibility of this scenario—in which reinforcing alerts by both nations propel them to war—is borne out by history. In 1914, the process of mobilizing and alerting European armies outran the control of political leaders and drew them, inevitably, into military confrontation.

The conditions that triggered World War I serve, according to some specialists, as an ominous blueprint for World War III. The enormous destructive power, short flight times, and high accuracy of modern nuclear weapons place new pressures on command systems that have grown more intricate, interdependent, and quick-reacting over time. As Bracken concludes, ". . . the danger facing the world is that the superpowers have institutionalized a major nuclear showdown."

Observations such as these, however grim and frightening, deserve thoughtful consideration by citizens and policymakers alike. Our full appreciation of the risks of war—and the difficulties of managing nuclear forces—may be the first step toward preventing disaster in the future.

■ Selected Sources

David P. Barash and Judith Eve Lipton, *Stop Nuclear War! A Handbook* (Grove Press, Inc., 1982).

Louis René Beres, *Apocalypse: Nuclear Catastrophe in World Politics* (The University of Chicago Press, 1980).

Richard K. Betts, *Surprise Attack* (The Brookings Institution, 1982).

Paul Bracken, *The Command and Control of Nuclear Forces* (Yale University Press, 1983).

Ground Zero, *Thinking About Preventing Nuclear War* (Ground Zero, 1982).

Richard Halloran, "Spread of Nuclear Weapons Is Seen by 2000," *The New York Times,* November 15, 1982.

———,"U.S. Fears Attacks on Nuclear Sites," *The New York Times,* October 23, 1982.

"Nuclear War by 1999?" *Harvard Magazine,* November 1975.

Bill Prochnau, "At the Crater's Edge" (Part 4), *The Washington Post,* April 28, 1982 (other articles in series appeared on April 25, 26, 27, 29, 30 and May 1, 1982).

David Schribman, "Experts Fear That Unpredictable Chain of Events Could Bring Nuclear War," *The New York Times,* June 24, 1982.

Ruth Leger Sivard, *World Military and Social Expenditures 1982* (World Priorities, 1982).

"U.S. Nuclear Weapons Accidents: Danger in Our Midst," *The Defense Monitor* (Center for Defense Information, 1981).

Can Deterrence Offer Security?

Surveying the nuclear threat offers grim evidence of our common peril and draws us to search for paths to security. Fear of nuclear war is "the most intelligent feeling of our time," writes Leon Wieseltier, a senior editor of *The New Republic*. "It animates the policymakers as well as the protesters. Who is *for* nuclear war?"

Since the end of World War II, military policy has been shaped by the existence of nuclear weapons and the desire to avoid their use. Unfortunately, the complex nature of nuclear weapons strategy and the abstract tenor of discussion among experts have defied understanding by most lay persons. Paul Warnke, Director of the Arms Control and Disarmament Agency in the Carter Administration, describes the problem of briefing a presidential candidate on this issue:

> I remember back when I was doing my best to get Ed Muskie nominated and elected. It must have been about 1970. At one point he asked me to talk to him about strategic arms and strategic nuclear doctrine. I did for about forty minutes, and I thought I was being extraordinarily eloquent. At the end of it, he looked at me and said, "You've got to be nuts." I think that's the general reaction people have.

Awakened to the risk of nuclear war, concerned citizens are beginning to probe the complicated realm of *nuclear doctrine*—those beliefs and values that shape official policy on nuclear arms. By acquainting ourselves with the language of weaponry and strategy, we can reconsider accepted dogma and examine the premises of policymakers responsible for national security.

■ Nuclear Weapons and National Security

There are many dimensions to national security, a phrase that connotes the vitality, well-being, and safety of a country. Traditionally, national security has been associated with defense—protecting a nation's people from physical harm. In this context, military force has been a primary means to guard against threats to national security.

Since the detonation of the first atomic bomb in 1945, military force has taken on a new meaning. The special characteristics of nuclear weapons distinguish them from non-nuclear, conventional armaments in two interrelated ways. First, nuclear weapons can cause unparalleled devastation to populations and homelands, reaching beyond the traditional confines of military battlefields. Second, they pose an inescapable threat to any areas that are targeted for attack. Retired Admiral Noel Gayler, former Director of the National Security Agency and former Commander of all U.S. forces in the Pacific, explains why shielding targets against nuclear weapons is extremely difficult:

> In conventional air defense, it's enough to shoot down a few aircraft at each go—the cumulative losses soon bring the attack to a halt. In nuclear defense, the situation is reversed: essentially all weapons have to be stopped or else the damage is done.

The nuclear age thus is characterized by twin perils: the extreme vulnerability of populations and the virtual impossibility of defense. When the United States held an atomic monopoly from 1945 to 1949, these conditions were regarded as military assets to be exploited, if necessary, in the name of security. Once the Soviet Union tested its first atomic bomb, American defense planners faced a difficult dilemma: the very weapons that had promised to serve our national interest now threatened our security and even our survival.

■ Designing a Nuclear Strategy

The prospect of a nuclear attack by the Soviet Union has shaped official thinking on the function and role of nuclear weapons in U.S. defense planning. Writing in the late 1940s, Bernard Brodie, a noted strategist at the Yale Center for International Studies, offered this timeless advice to military leaders:

> The first and most vital step in the American security program for the age of atomic bombs is to take measures to guarantee ourselves in case of attack the possibility of retaliation in kind.
>
> Thus far the chief purpose of a military establishment has been to win wars. From now on its chief purpose must be to avoid them. It can have no other useful purpose.

Brodie's classic prescription rested on three basic assumptions:

- that the use of nuclear weapons by an adversary must be discouraged;
- that the best way to discourage their use is by threatening nuclear punishment; and
- that the purpose of nuclear weapons is to dissuade the other side from using theirs.

Loopholes in Deterrence?

Nuclear deterrence, to a large extent, is rooted in the art of persuasion. According to deterrence theory, a potential aggressor faced with the prospect of retaliation will be dissuaded from initiating a nuclear attack. This strategy presumes that leaders are sufficiently rational to appreciate the "costs" of nuclear war and are sufficiently in control of events to exercise their judgment.

Many observers fear that these two factors—rationality and control—are at odds with the real world. During a period of political crisis, the occurrence of false alarms, terrorist activity, or weapons accidents could tax nuclear command structures in unpredictable ways. Moreover, in an actual military emergency, the pressures on government leaders would be enormous. As Stanford University President Donald Kennedy observes:

> . . . no chief of state, no government official, no senior military officer behaves like a "rational actor" in making decisions when the fate of nations and the world hangs in the balance. . . . Rationality will be especially hard to conserve in the early stages of a nuclear conflict, where uncertainty and the need for rapid decisions dominate. That is why it seems so unlikely to experienced military leaders as well as to others that a nuclear war can ever remain limited.

Over the past three decades, these assumptions have become an integral part of U.S. strategic doctrine, embodied in a concept known as *deterrence*. In general terms, the theory of deterrence presupposes that one country will not attack another if the prospective cost of the action is perceived to outweigh any potential gain. This approach, a traditional part of military thinking, gains particular force in a world of nuclear-armed adversaries, where the stakes of confrontation are tremendously high.

In his article "How Not to Think About Nuclear War," author Theodore Draper offers this explanation of nuclear deterrence:

> Deterrence is another way of saying that nuclear weapons will not be abolished and will not be used. If they were abolished, there would be no need to deter their use. But they will not be used because they could annihilate both sides using them. It would concentrate the mind wonderfully to hold on firmly to what pure and simple deterrence means.

Most, if not all, U.S. military thinkers agree on the general definition of nuclear deterrence. There are disagreements, however, on the implications of deterrence for policy planning. Three basic questions form the core of this debate:

- What types of threatened punishment will discourage nuclear attack?
- What weapons and targets are necessary to support those threats?
- What plans should be made for using nuclear weapons in the event an attack occurs?

In recent literature on nuclear strategy, these key issues generally are phrased as "What deters?" and "What happens if deterrence fails?" To date, American military and civilian officials have relied on two competing schools of thought for answers to these questions. Donald Snow, author of *Nuclear Strategy in a Dynamic World,* characterizes the leading philosophies as the "deterrence-only" position, associated with the threat of assured destruction, and the "deterrence-plus" position, associated with the threat of nuclear war-fighting.

Over the past 30 years, each of these approaches has been accorded varying degrees of emphasis in public statements of American policy. Both, however, represent abstractions rather than complete descriptions of actual strategic doctrine at any point in history. Nevertheless, the debate over nuclear deterrence is most easily understood in the context of these two viewpoints. A comparison of assured destruction and nuclear war-fighting reveals competing theories about the nature of nuclear war and the role of nuclear weapons in preventing its occurrence.

The Threat of Assured Destruction

"At the heart of American defense policy," writes author Thomas Powers in *The Atlantic Monthly,* "is a theory of what a big modern war might be like, and how we ought to fight it." The phrase *assured destruction*—coined in 1964 by then-Secretary of Defense Robert McNamara—emphasizes the disastrous nature of nuclear war as a cataclysmic event that would destroy both American and Soviet societies. In the words of McNamara, "No meaningful victory is even conceivable in a third unlimited world war, for no nation can possibly win a full-scale thermonuclear exchange."

Given these realities, the theory of assured destruction—commonly known as *mutual assured destruction,* or *MAD*—presumes that a nation will refrain from initiating nuclear war because of its self-interest in survival. "What deters" is the risk that any use of nuclear arms, however limited, will be met with a devastating response by one's adversary.

The Logic of Assured Destruction

Three principles, embodied in MAD, are designed to reinforce the doctrine of deterrence. First, the threat of nuclear punishment is mutual. Each population, vulnerable to nuclear attack, is held "hostage" to the other.

Second, the prospect of nuclear punishment is assured. Regardless of the damage that might be sustained from its enemy's initial attack, each country possesses sufficient nuclear weapons to guarantee retaliation. That is, each side has the military capability to carry out its threat.

Finally, the threatened punishment—destruction—is so severe that the cost of nuclear aggression outweighs any possible gains. Rational leaders thus are deterred from hostile acts by the prospect of unacceptable losses to their homeland.

Ultimately, the success of MAD as a U.S. defense strategy depends on whether our threat of punishment is credible to the Soviet Union. Soviet leaders genuinely must believe—or at least think it probable—that the United States is able and willing to destroy their homeland in response to a nuclear attack. Over the years, American military planners have taken several actions to reinforce the threat of assured destruction. First, the United States has acquired a secure *second-strike* arsenal of nuclear weapons—forces that can survive a nuclear attack in sufficient numbers to guarantee retaliation. Second, the United States has retained the ability to inflict what we think would be unacceptable damage on Soviet society in the event of an all-out war. This capability includes the capacity for *countervalue targeting*—striking directly at Soviet cities, factories, mines, and other "value centers."

Deterring War in Europe

Public discussion of deterrence usually centers on the prospect of a Soviet nuclear attack on the United States. Official policy, as commonly understood, promises that the United States will use its nuclear weapons in retaliation to a Soviet strategic strike on American territory.

Yet much of the recent debate over deterrence centers on the particular problem of deterring war against allies of the United States. This lesser-known aspect of U.S. nuclear doctrine, termed *extended deterrence,* calls for the use of nuclear weapons to deter a Soviet attack on Europe or Japan. Several factors distinguish this strategy from the popular view of deterrence:

- It extends the "nuclear shield" of the United States beyond American soil to foreign territory;
- It seeks to deter *conventional* as well as nuclear attack on our allies by the Soviet Union; and
- It commits the United States to use nuclear weapons *first* if conventional arms are judged insufficient against Soviet conventional forces.

Extended deterrence is rooted in the presumption that nuclear weapons can bolster the defense of the Western alliance, organized under the North Atlantic Treaty Organization (NATO). Concern about the disparity between NATO's conventional forces and those of the Soviet-East European alliance, known as the Warsaw Pact, has given

These tactics, according to MAD's proponents, give operational meaning to the doctrine of deterrence and credence to the threat of nuclear punishment.

Political scientist Robert Jervis summarizes the logic of assured destruction as the basis for nuclear strategy:

> Because a military advantage no longer assures a decisive victory, old ways of thinking are no longer appropriate. The healthy fear of devastation . . . makes deterrence relatively easy. Furthermore, because cities cannot be taken out of hostage, the perceived danger of total destruction is crucial at all points in the threat, display, or use of force.

The "healthy fear of devastation" and the "perceived danger of total destruction" have proven, not surprisingly, to be controversial underpinnings for U.S. policy. At issue are several disparate yet critical concerns relating to the viability of assured destruction as a strategy for preventing nuclear war.

The Limits of Assured Destruction

Over time, people have come to question MAD as a basis for U.S. nuclear policy. Their reservations center on three issues: the magnitude of the punishment, the morality of the threat, and the flexibility of the strategy for military planning.

Most observers are reconciled to the deterrent role of nuclear weapons, given their very existence and awesome capacity for damage. Nevertheless, many decry the potential for "overkill" represented by current arsenals. As arms control expert Spurgeon Keeny, Jr., and physicist Wolfgang Panofsky observe:

> A devastating attack on the urban societies of the United States and the Soviet Union would in fact require only a very small fraction of the more than 50,000 nuclear weapons currently in the arsenals of the two superpowers.

Given this fact, a number of individuals are persuaded by the logic of *minimal deterrence* as a guide for nuclear strategy. They maintain that smaller arsenals aimed at fewer targets pose a sufficient threat of nuclear punishment. Lord Solly Zuckerman, the former chief scientific advisor to the British Ministry of Defense, writes:

> It seem[s] . . . inconceivable that in a rational world any country would try to further some aggressive aim if the risk were the total destruction of its own capital city, let alone that of its ten largest cities.

Other observers, however, condemn the targeting of *any* population centers—a moral objection raised by the National Conference of Catholic Bishops:

> Under no circumstances may nuclear weapons or other instruments of mass slaughter be used for the purpose

of destroying population centers.

Retaliatory action which would indiscriminately take many wholly innocent lives, lives of people who are in no way responsible for reckless actions of their government, must also be condemned. This condemnation, in our judgment, applies even to the retaliatory use of weapons striking enemy cities after our own have already been struck.

Reliance on the threat of assured destruction thus creates an ethical dilemma for many individuals, leading some to renounce mutual deterrence altogether and others to tolerate it as a stop-gap measure only.

Frustration with the "all or nothing" tenor of MAD is shared by a markedly different school of critics—those concerned with waging a "limited" nuclear war. Writing in 1974, defense analyst Albert Wohlstetter argued:

We cannot assure that a nuclear war will never occur simply by repeating that it would be an unlimited catastrophe. And we cannot eliminate the possibility of nuclear war simply by *assuring* that if it occurs it *will* be an unlimited catastrophe.

According to this view, a strategy based on MAD is too inflexible and locks the United States into a "suicide pact." The threat of a massive response to any level of nuclear aggression may tie the hands of national leaders and invite counterretaliation in kind. Moreover, this suicidal posture may appear incredible to nuclear adversaries contemplating a small-scale attack. Given these concerns, some observers maintain that MAD jeopardizes deterrence and offers little guidance for military planning if deterrence fails. The alternative, they say, is a strategy based on the threat of nuclear war-fighting.

The Threat of Nuclear War-fighting

The concept of *nuclear war-fighting* is known by many names, such as *limited nuclear options, flexible nuclear response,* and the *Schlesinger doctrine,* due to its strong association with James Schlesinger, Secretary of Defense in the Nixon and Ford Administrations. At the heart of this strategy is the belief that the use of nuclear weapons need not be catastrophic, that the outbreak of nuclear war could occur in a variety of ways, and that a limited or prolonged war is a more likely form of confrontation than a massive, cataclysmic exchange between adversaries.

Given this view, war-fighting theorists maintain that nuclear weapons can be used "selectively"—in proportion to the nature and level of Soviet aggression. "What deters," explains author Donald Snow, is the prospect of "denying the

rise to this controversial *first-use* policy. At issue are several questions that highlight the tension between assured destruction and nuclear war-fighting: How credible is the American threat to use nuclear weapons against Soviet forces in Europe? Should the defense of Europe depend on risking its survival in a nuclear exchange? Can nuclear war be limited to Europe? In threatening the Soviet Union, does the United States invite preemption or retaliation against American territory? Must the protection of American interests abroad involve the risk of full-scale nuclear war? Concern about this risk is leading some observers—notably McGeorge Bundy, George Kennan, Robert McNamara, Gerard Smith, and others—to call for NATO to adopt a policy of *no-first-use,* a strategy not to use nuclear weapons in Europe, or anywhere else, except in response to a nuclear attack. Ultimately, the debate over no-first-use will test the viability of deterrence theory—the notion that nuclear weapons can serve no purpose other than the *prevention* of their use. •

enemy a specific objective, rather than punishing the enemy indiscriminately." Secretary Schlesinger's 1975 report to Congress discussed the rationale for this approach to deterrence:

> . . . a massive retaliation against cities, in response to anything less than an all-out attack on the U.S. and its cities, appears less and less credible. . . . What we need is a series of measured responses which bear some relation to the provocation, have the prospect of terminating hostilities before general nuclear war breaks out, and leave some possibility for restoring deterrence.

The Logic of Nuclear War-fighting

Schlesinger's guidelines for "restoring deterrence" reflect three basic assumptions about military strategy. First, a strategy based on assured destruction creates a dangerous dilemma for national leaders: "Should a President, in the event of nuclear attack, be left with the single option of ordering the mass destruction of enemy civilians, in the face of the certainty that it would be followed by the mass slaughter of Americans?" This problem, raised in President Nixon's 1970 foreign policy report to Congress, purportedly can be eased if graduated means of nuclear retaliation are at hand.

Accordingly, the theory of nuclear war-fighting emphasizes the value of *intrawar deterrence*—a strategy that compels the enemy to back down by emphasizing the potential for further harm. Such coercion depends on a capacity for *counterforce targeting*—attacking the enemy's nuclear forces and other sources of military strength. By threatening to match the enemy blow for blow, this strategy is intended to deter aggression with a credible response short of all-out war. Should nuclear war occur, counterforce targeting is intended to contain hostilities by persuading the enemy that further conflict is against its interests. This objective, known as *escalation control,* is described by Michael May of the Lawrence Livermore National Laboratory:

> The main usefulness of nuclear weapons, if we are attacked, will be to make sure that the attacker is prevented from following up his attack with steps that would lead to further destruction or domination of this country and its allies.

Finally, nuclear war-fighting, unlike assured destruction, offers the hope of a favorable outcome to nuclear warfare, a notion developed by defense analyst Herman Kahn in his famous 1960 treatise, *On Thermonuclear War:*

> Once one accepts the idea that deterrence is not absolutely reliable and that it would be possible to survive a war, then [one] may be willing to buy insurance—to spend money on preparations to . . . limit damage, facilitate recuperation, and to get the best military result

possible—at least "to prevail" in some meaningful sense if you cannot win.

According to war-fighting theorists, American nuclear forces must be able to injure the Soviet Union short of total destruction to succeed in this mixed mission of deterrence and escalation control. Until 1974, U.S. nuclear attack plans called for launching, at a minimum, 2,500 weapons against Soviet nuclear forces—"a blow so enormous," notes author Thomas Powers, "that it virtually guaranteed an all-out response." Since then, preparations for nuclear war-fighting have been expanded by the Nixon, Carter, and Reagan Administrations in several significant ways:

- to provide options for limited nuclear strikes against selected targets;
- to maintain a reserve of U.S. nuclear weapons for protection and coercion during and after major nuclear conflict; and
- to emphasize targets key to Soviet retaliatory and recovery capabilities, including its nuclear arsenal, war-related industry, and political and bureaucratic apparatus.

These tactics were endorsed most recently in the *Defense Guidance* paper issued by Defense Secretary Caspar Weinberger in 1982 to help the military services plan their forces for the next five years. Weinberger's stated objective is for American nuclear forces to be capable of controlled nuclear counterattacks over a protracted period:

... should deterrence fail and strategic nuclear war with the U.S.S.R. occur, the United States must prevail and be able to force the Soviet Union to seek earliest termination of the hostilities on terms favorable to the United States.

This statement has triggered a new round of public debate over nuclear war-fighting—and war-winning—strategies. In defense of the Administration's policy, one Pentagon official offered this statement to reporters:

The important thing to bear in mind here is that no one is suggesting in this guidance that a protracted [nuclear] war is a good thing, a desirable thing, something that we want to do, something that we are planning to do. But the capability of dealing with a protracted attack upon us is important to develop, because if we develop the capability . . . we can hope to deter it.

Despite these assurances, many experts question the viability of nuclear war-fighting as a strategy for deterrence.

The Limits of Nuclear War-fighting

The main arguments against war-fighting plans center on two basic issues: Does preparing for nuclear war make it more likely to occur? Can nuclear war be controlled once it begins?

A central theme of nuclear war-fighting is counterforce targeting, which, although geared toward deterrence, may be highly suggestive of *first-strike* intentions—a willingness to initiate a nuclear attack aimed at disarming the enemy and precluding retaliation. Faced with a first-strike threat, a nation is likely to respond in one of several ways. It may develop its own counterforce capability to match the enemy's—triggering a new round in the arms race. It may adopt a policy of *launch on warning,* preparing to launch its missiles upon receipt of signals that enemy missiles are en route to its territory. This practice not only is susceptible to false alarms but also places nuclear weapons on a "hair trigger" response. Or a nation may consider the more drastic step of a *preemptive strike,* that is, firing its own weapons first at the onset of hostilities on the assumption that enemy attack is imminent. Such extreme measures reflect the pressures created by counterforce targeting to fire one's weapons before they are destroyed—to "use 'em or lose 'em" in a crisis.

Moreover, counterforce war plans mask the moral dilemma of targeting civilian populations, thus reducing inhibitions against the use of nuclear weapons. Even the "side effects" of surgical strikes on military targets, however, would cause massive human suffering and death. This fact is recognized in the pastoral letter of the National Conference of Catholic Bishops:

> We are told that some weapons are designed for purely "counterforce" use against military forces and targets. The moral issue, however, is not resolved by the design of weapons or the planned intention for use; there are also consequences which must be assessed. It would be a perverted political policy or moral causistry which tried to justify using a weapon which "indirectly" or "unintentionally" killed a million innocent people because they happened to live near a "militarily significant target."

Concern about war-fighting strategies are also raised in the context of escalation control. Many observers question the presumption that selective nuclear strikes will demonstrate resolve and induce the enemy to back down. "[D]oubtless the other side hopes the same of us," notes Thomas Powers in his article, "Choosing a Strategy for World War III." Herbert Scoville, Jr., President of the Arms Control Association and former CIA Deputy Director for Science and Technology, is equally skeptical of this strategy: "No one knows how to stop a nuclear war because no one knows how to lose."

According to this view, the desire to prevail at all levels of hostilities may generate limitless requirements for nuclear weapons that subtly reduce inhibitions against their use. Moreover, the threat of retaliation may invite counterretaliation, creating inevitable pressures for escalation that offset the prospect for intrawar deterrence. As political scientist Robert Jervis points out, such war-fighting strategies may be self-defeating and cause deterrence to fail:

> . . . to develop a posture based on the assumption that limited nuclear wars are possible is to increase the chance that they will occur. If the Russians already believe in the possibility that such wars could be kept limited, U.S. acceptance of this position would increase the likelihood of their occurrence. On the other hand, if the Russians now find these kinds of war incomprehensible, they might learn to accept them if the United States talked about them long and persuasively enough. This could decrease the chance that a nuclear war would immediately involve the mass destruction of population centers, but at the cost of increasing the chance of more limited nuclear wars—which then could escalate.

Jervis' statement reflects the dilemma of nuclear deterrence—its inherent reliance on chance, on assumptions, and on perceptions of risk. "This legion of uncertainties," writes British defense scholar Lawrence Freedman, "ought to have created a common humility—to be so much in the dark with so much at stake. Unfortunately the frustration with this predicament led many strategists to show astonishing confidence in their own nostrums . . . ."

Today, public debate over competing deterrence theories must be tempered by a recognition of their limitations and lack of guarantees. What we *do* know, however, is that any use of nuclear weapons poses a grave risk of escalating beyond control. Moreover, recent scientific studies suggest that even a limited strike could be suicidal to the nation launching it, given the dire, long-term climactic effects of nuclear explosions. These are the realities of nuclear warfare that challenge any view of nuclear weapons as other than unmanageable tools of destruction.

◼ Selected Sources

McGeorge Bundy, George F. Kennan, Robert S. McNamara, and Gerard Smith, "Nuclear Weapons and the Atlantic Alliance," *Foreign Affairs,* Spring 1982.

Theodore Draper, "How Not to Think about Nuclear War," *The New York Review of Books,* July 15, 1982.

Lawrence Freedman, *The Evolution of Nuclear Strategy* (St. Martin's Press, 1981).

Robert Jervis, *"What Deters? The Ability to Inflict Assured Destruction,"* in *American Defense Policy,* edited by John F. Reichart and Steven R. Sturm (The Johns Hopkins University Press, 1982).

Spurgeon M. Keeny, Jr. and Wolfgang K.H. Panofsky, "MAD vs. NUTS: The Mutual Hostage Relationship of the Superpowers," *Foreign Affairs,* Winter 1981/1982.

The National Conference of Catholic Bishops, *The Challenge of Peace: God's Promise and Our Response,* May 3, 1983.

Thomas Powers, "Choosing a Strategy for World War III," *The Atlantic Monthly,* November 1982.

———, *Thinking About Nuclear War* (Alfred A. Knopf, 1982).

Donald M. Snow, *Nuclear Strategy in a Dynamic World: American Policy in the 1980s* (The University of Alabama Press, 1981).

Lawrence D. Weiler, "No First Use: A History," *Bulletin of the Atomic Scientists,* February 1983.

Leon Wieseltier, "Nuclear War, Nuclear Peace," *The New Republic,* January 10 and 17, 1983 (special issue).

Solly Zuckerman, *Nuclear Illusion and Reality* (The Viking Press, 1982).

II. WHAT IS THE NUCLEAR BALANCE OF FORCES?

The debate over who is ahead has lost all perspective as the players have forgotten the catastrophic damage that even a few nuclear explosions can produce.

Herbert Scoville, Jr.
Former Deputy Director for
Science and Technology,
Central Intelligence Agency
1981

How Do U.S. and Soviet Nuclear Forces Compare?

Almost any speech or newspaper article on nuclear arms control contains some reference to the U.S. and Soviet "strategic balance." Citizens are barraged with conflicting messages that the balance is "precarious," the balance is "favorable," or the balance is "irrelevant." But few citizens have an adequate frame of reference for evaluating such claims.

There are, to be sure, innumerable charts and graphs offering visual scorecards of the nuclear arms race. Yet even these summaries are difficult to interpret. They typically are riddled with complex terms—throw-weight, equivalent megatonnage, and the like—that defy common understanding. They also are incomplete, measuring certain aspects of nuclear weaponry without addressing others. And they are vulnerable, like any statistics, to manipulation and misinterpretation.

Alerted to these pitfalls, concerned citizens can pierce the smokescreen of numbers that has clouded public debate over nuclear arms policy. We can ask not only "Who's ahead?" but "What does 'ahead' mean?" in the context of current efforts to prevent nuclear war.

■ The Meaning of the Balance

The comparative strength of U.S. and Soviet nuclear forces is commonly described as the *nuclear balance*. Discussions of the *strategic* nuclear balance, like the one that follows, center on the relative capability of each superpower to destroy the other's territory, its heartland of military, political, and economic strength.

In surveying the strategic balance, there is a popular tendency to seek reassurance that the United States is ahead, that we are "winning" the nuclear arms race. According to many observers, this preoccupation with strategic advantage is misplaced, given the staggering size of current arsenals and their capacity for damage. In a much quoted statement, Henry Kissinger, Secretary of State in the Nixon and Ford Administrations, remarked at a 1974 press conference:

> . . . what in the name of God is strategic superiority? What is the significance of it, politically, militarily, operationally at these levels of numbers? What do you do with it?

Similarly, retired Admiral Noel Gayler, former Director of the National Security Agency, wrote in 1982:

> In the real world, "superiority" has no meaning. We and Russia are like two riverboat gamblers sitting across a green table, each with a gun pointed at the other's belly and each gun on hair trigger. The size of the guns doesn't make much difference; if either weapon is used, both gamblers are dead.

Despite such compelling messages, current military planning often is shaped by the "numbers fallacy," a practice that former Chairman of the Joint Chiefs of Staff Maxwell Taylor dubs "keeping up with the Russian Joneses." This line of reasoning not only determines what weapons programs are promoted and funded, but which arms control initiatives are pursued, and how national security ultimately is defined. Given the importance of these policy issues, informed citizen participation demands a basic understanding of U.S. and Soviet nuclear arsenals and an appreciation of their similarities and differences.*

◼ Measuring the Strategic Balance

Measuring the strategic balance is a complicated task. There are many ways to compare U.S. and Soviet long-range nuclear forces, but there is no consensus on which are the most significant comparisons or how they should be weighed. This chapter surveys the most common indicators of U.S. and Soviet strategic strength: static measures of peacetime nuclear capabilities—the numbers, power, and characteristics of nuclear weapons forces—and dynamic measures of how these forces might interact in a nuclear war.

Comparing Numbers of Weapons

Numerical comparisons of U.S. and Soviet nuclear arsenals are frequently used because they are simple to compute and easy to understand. The preoccupation of arms control with numerical limits on weapons has reinforced the tendency to "bean count"—to evaluate the relative strength of superpower forces by tallying the quantity of weapons on each side. Common quantitative measures of nuclear capability include the numbers of strategic delivery vehicles, strategic launchers, and strategic warheads.*

Counting the total number of *strategic delivery vehicles*

---

*The effect of future technological developments on the strategic balance is discussed in Chapter 6, "How Will New Technology Affect the Risk of Nuclear War?"

*Comparing Numbers: Key Terms**

Strategic delivery vehicles are vehicles that can deliver nuclear explosive devices to targets over intercontinental distances. The term specifically refers to long-range ballistic missiles and strategic nuclear-armed aircraft.

A ***ballistic missile*** moves toward its target in an arc-like path under the influence of gravity after a brief period of powered flight. There are two types of long-range ballistic missiles: ***intercontinental ballistic missiles (ICBMs)*** are based on the continental United States and have sufficient range to attack most or all of the Soviet Union (Soviet ICBMs have corresponding capability); ***submarine-launched ballistic missiles (SLBMs)*** are transported by and launched from nuclear submarines.

Strategic nuclear aircraft include two types of nuclear-armed bombers, which generally are differentiated as follows: ***heavy bombers*** with intercontinental range, and ***medium bombers*** that lack *(continued)*

---

*These definitions, and those that follow, are based on information from four sources: *A Glossary of Arms Control Terms*, prepared by the Arms Control Association; *SALT II Glossary of Terms*, prepared by the U.S. Arms Control and Disarmament Agency; the report of the *President's Commission on Strategic Forces* (the Scowcroft Commission); and *U.S.-Soviet Military Balance: Concepts and Capabilities 1960-1980* by John M. Collins.

round-trip intercontinental range without in-flight refueling but are suitable for strategic bombing on one-way missions.

Strategic launchers are the equipment required to launch missiles. The term refers to bombers (in the case of bomber-carried weapons); missile tubes on submarines (in the case of SLBMs); and land-based equipment such as silo launchers (in the case of ICBMs housed in vertical, underground installations). A single ballistic missile can carry **Multiple Independently-targetable Re-entry Vehicles (MIRVs),** a package of two or more re-entry vehicles which can be delivered to separate targets. The **re-entry vehicle** is the part of the missile that carries the explosive device and re-enters the earth's atmosphere in the last phase of flight. The explosive device is called the **nuclear warhead,** the part of the missile or other munition that explodes and causes damage to the target.   •

indicates which nation leads in missiles and bombers—a straightforward way of comparing U.S. and Soviet nuclear forces. A similar and often preferred basis for comparison is *strategic launchers.* Launching equipment, such as silos, is more difficult to conceal than the missiles themselves, hence easier to count and monitor.

Both measures have only limited significance, however, as yardsticks of strategic strength. Most importantly, they fail to reflect the fact that a single missile or bomber may be equipped with more than one nuclear weapon. *MIRVed* delivery systems can carry several nuclear warheads, each of which can be aimed at a separate target. Moreover, a single launcher may sometimes be capable of firing more than one missile in sequence.

Given these factors, statistics on delivery vehicles and launchers can understate a nation's nuclear capability. They reveal which side is equipped to launch more missiles and bombers but not which side can deliver more warheads to enemy targets.

Strategic Launchers*

	United States	Soviet Union
ICBM launchers	1,049	1,398
SLBM launchers	520	969
Bombers	328	245
Total	**1,897**	**2,612**

Counting the total number of *strategic warheads* indicates how many deliverable bombs each side has and how many targets each side theoretically can hit. This statistic is widely regarded as the most useful quantitative yardstick of nuclear capability: "I consider this [warheads] to be the most important measure of relative strength," says Hans Bethe, former Director of the Theoretical Physics Division of the Los Alamos Scientific Laboratory. Nevertheless, counting warheads is subject to some imprecision. Certain missiles and bombers may be deployed or readied for use with a variety of modifications that affect the amount of explosives they carry. As a result, current estimates on warheads reflect assumptions about the types and numbers of weapons that are operational on each side.

*Statistics on U.S. and Soviet nuclear forces, unless otherwise noted, are based on information from a document prepared by the Congressional Research Service: *U.S./Soviet Military Balance: Statistical Trends, 1970-1982* (October 1981, updated August 1, 1983) by John M. Collins.

Strategic Warheads

	United States	Soviet Union
ICBM warheads	2,149	5,862
SLBM warheads	4,800	1,865
Bomber-carried weapons	2,626	345
Total	**9,575**	**8,072**

In Perspective: A Ground Zero publication, Nuclear War: What's In It For You?, *reminds us that "a single missile can deliver a warhead whose explosive power surpasses that of all of the 2.2 million tons of bombs dropped on Germany in World War II."*

In sum, numerical comparisons of U.S. and Soviet strategic forces indicate a Soviet advantage in strategic delivery vehicles and launchers and a U.S. lead in deliverable warheads. But such generalizations, however interesting, reveal limited information about the overall state of the strategic balance. They answer the popular inquiry "Whose arsenal is larger?" but not "Whose arsenal is stronger?"—a question that involves both quantitative and qualitative judgments about the relative strength of each side's force.

Comparing Destructive Power

Comparisons of destructive power are intended to measure the so-called *military potential* of U.S. and Soviet strategic nuclear forces. Current debate over the purposes of nuclear weapons—as retaliatory instruments of mass destruction or as selective war-fighting tools—has focused attention on the lethal effects of each side's arsenal. Common yardsticks of destructive capability include throw-weight, yield, and accuracy.

Comparing *throw-weight,* that is, the lift capacity of a missile, is a common way of quantifying destructive capability. The "heavier" the missile, the more weight it can lift off the ground and the more warheads it can carry to a target. Figures on missile throw-weight and *bomber payload* represent the total weight of nuclear cargo that one nation can deliver against an opponent.

Throw-weight can be misleading, however, as an index of strength. For example, this measure fails to take account of technological developments, such as the miniaturization of guidance computers and warheads, that reduce the weight of a missile's contents. Moreover, there is a less-than-proportional relationship between the pounds a missile carries and the explosive power of its warheads. Given these fac-

Comparing Destructive Power: Key Terms

Throw-weight refers to lift capacity—the poundage a missile can lift into a flight path and carry to a target. It describes the maximum weight of the re-entry vehicles, the targeting devices (or guidance system), the decoy equipment, and other mechanical gear. A related term, ***payload,*** refers to the weapon and/or cargo capacity of any aircraft or missile system, also expressed in pounds.

Yield refers to the force of a nuclear explosion expressed as the equivalent of the energy produced by tons of TNT. One ***kiloton (1 kt)*** and one ***megaton (1 mt)*** nuclear warheads have respective yields of one thousand and one million tons of TNT. (The weapon used on Hiroshima was a relatively small one with about 14 kilotons of explosive force.)

Accuracy refers to the ability of warheads to land near their intended targets. It is measured in terms of ***circular error probable (CEP),*** that is, the radius of a circle around a target—often expressed in feet or meters—in which half of the warheads aimed at the target will land. •

tors, defense journalist Fred Kaplan notes, "Bigness is beside the point," and crude throw-weight comparisons offer limited information about strategic strength.

Throw-weight (total missile and heavy bomber cargo)

United States	Soviet Union
7.2 million pounds	11.8 million pounds

In Perspective: As Lord Solly Zuckerman, author of Nuclear Illusion and Reality, *observes, "Today, ten times, a hundred times, the amount of explosive power that wiped out Hiroshima and Nagasaki can be packed in a single warhead weighing less than a fifth of either of the first two nuclear devices."*

Source: Department of Defense Annual Report Fiscal Year 1981

Comparing total *yield* is another means of assessing nuclear capability. Statistics on total megatonnage indicate which side has more "firepower" to deliver against enemy targets.

Increasing the megatonnage of weapons, however, does not necessarily increase their lethality. Destruction does not increase proportionally with a simple increase in yield; for example, a two-megaton warhead is not twice as destructive as a one-megaton warhead.* Beyond a certain point, additional yield is superfluous in terms of the devastation it can wreak on a given target and the surrounding area. Accordingly, statistics on raw explosive power are a useful but incomplete basis for comparing the destructive capability of U.S. and Soviet nuclear arsenals.

Yield (total warheads and bombs)

United States	Soviet Union
3448 megatons	4535 megatons

In Perspective: Dr. H. Jack Geiger of Physicians for Social Responsibility explains, "At one megaton—a small weapon by contemporary standards—we are trying to imagine 70 simultaneous Hiroshima explosions. At 20 megatons we are trying to imagine 1,400 Hiroshima bombs detonated at the same moment in the same place."

Source: The Arms Race and Arms Control by the Stockholm International Peace Research Institute (1982)

---

*A related measure, *equivalent megatonnage*, takes into account the fact that small nuclear weapons do proportionally more damage than large ones.

Accuracy is at least as important as yield in determining destructive capability. As Thomas Powers, author of *Thinking About the Next War,* observes, "It is accuracy which determines the efficacy of violence in war . . . a particular blow on a particular spot . . . ." In the context of nuclear weapons, the combination of accuracy and yield determine the ultimate *lethality* of any warhead, that is, its ability to destroy an assigned target. As a general rule, the closer a warhead comes to a target, the less explosive power it must wield to succeed in its mission.

The devastation of large, unprotected targets such as cities, factories, or airfields—known as *soft* or *area* targets—does not require much precision. A 100-kt warhead could miss by a quarter mile and still inflict enormous damage. Against missile silos and command centers that are reinforced with concrete—known as *hard* or *point* targets—pinpoint accuracy as well as yield is important. In fact, a two-fold improvement in accuracy will have the same effect as an eight-fold improvement in yield.

Lethality generally is expressed in terms of *hard target kill potential,* a measurement of each nation's ability to destroy the other side's most protected nuclear forces. A further refinement of this yardstick is *time-urgent hard target kill potential,* which factors in the capability to strike enemy missile silos promptly, before any retaliatory weapons can be launched from them. Land-based ballistic missiles, with their flight times of 30 minutes, have this potential; bombers, taking 10 hours to cross continents, do not.

Comparing lethality is considered the ultimate way of assessing each side's military potential. Nevertheless, such comparisons are inevitably imprecise because they depend on estimates of missile accuracy. "Of all the characteristics of strategic weapons systems, accuracy is one of the hardest to predict," writes the International Institute for Strategic Studies, a London-based information center on military forces and security developments. Calculations of *circular error probable (CEP),* a measure of weapon precision, are subject to many uncertainties—a problem described in detail by MIT physicist Kosta Tsipis and student Matthew Bunn in a 1983 *Scientific American* article. CEP estimates, for example, are based on missile tests that are conducted on a very small scale, are difficult to interpret, and cannot simulate such variables as the influence of atmospheric conditions on re-entry or the gravitational effect of firing missiles on untested flight paths. Accordingly, projections of weapon accuracy should be read only as rough estimates of each side's capability to destroy enemy targets.

Accuracy

United States	Soviet Union
• greater accuracy • more hard target kill potential	• more time-urgent hard target kill potential

In Perspective: Author Thomas Powers writes, "The first nuclear weapons were a kind of mighty hammer, vast in power but hard to aim accurately. Now missiles can be dropped right down into Yankee Stadium from the other side of the planet."

In sum, comparisons of destructive power indicate that the Soviet Union leads in total yield, throw-weight, and prompt hard target kill potential. On the other hand, the United States has an advantage in accuracy and overall hard target capability.

These dissimilarities stem from differences in the kinds of weapons systems on which each side most relies. It is important, therefore, to examine the mix of nuclear forces in both the U.S. and Soviet strategic arsenals.

Comparing Kinds of Weapons

Comparisons of *force structure*—the kinds of nuclear weapons available to each superpower—are designed to offer a well-rounded picture of the strategic balance. "If you're trying to decide what the overall balance is, it is critical not to look at a narrow piece of the spectrum," explains Walter Slocombe, Deputy Under Secretary of Defense for Policy Planning in the Carter Administration.

The major components of U.S. and Soviet nuclear forces —*strategic bombers, intercontinental ballistic missiles (ICBMs)* and *submarine-launched ballistic missiles (SLBMs)*— are distinguished by certain traits that have a direct bearing on their capabilities. These characteristics include the ability to destroy targets ("lethality"), the ability to survive surprise attack ("survivability"), the ability to penetrate enemy defenses ("penetrability"), and the ability to receive and respond to command ("controllability").

Strategic Bombers

Both the United States and the Soviet Union relied on bombers to convey their nuclear weapons until the 1960s, when land- and sea-based ballistic missiles were deployed in large numbers. Since then, the evolution of U.S. and Soviet arsenals has diverged in terms of each side's relative emphasis on nuclear-armed aircraft. The U.S. strategic force, commonly described as a *triad,* involves all three military services and gives weight to each "leg": air (bombers), land (ICBMs), and sea (SLBMs). By contrast, the Soviet force is composed largely of ICBMs and SLBMs, with a markedly smaller bomber force. Accordingly, comparisons of U.S. and Soviet bombers reflect a fundamental difference in overall force structure.

The United States has 328 strategic nuclear aircraft. This force consists of B-52 heavy bombers and FB-111 medium bombers. The aircraft carry a total of 2,626 deliverable weapons, comprising some 27 percent of all U.S. strategic weapons. These include gravity bombs that can be dropped directly on targets as well as guided missiles launched from aircraft, either short-range attack missiles or long-range airlaunched cruise missiles.

The Soviet Union has 245 strategic nuclear aircraft. This force consists of Bear and Bison heavy bombers and Backfire medium bombers. The aircraft carry a total of 345 deliverable weapons, comprising only 4 percent of all Soviet strategic weapons.

Size of Bomber Forces

	United States	**Soviet Union**
Bombers	328	245
Bomber-carried weapons	2,626	345
(as percent of total warheads)	(27%)	(4%)

Several qualitative factors should be considered in assessing the contribution of bombers to the arsenals of the United States and the Soviet Union.

Bomber controllability: The greatest advantage of manned bombers is the ability of their crews to follow directions after launch. Unlike computer-guided missiles, U.S. and Soviet aircraft can be called back, retargeted, or dispersed upon receiving in-flight instructions from national authorities. This is a key reason why the U.S. Joint Chiefs of Staff consider bombers "the most flexible component of the Triad."

Bomber penetrability: The mobility and flexibility of aircraft allow them to penetrate enemy territory in an unpredictable manner and deliver bombs in a variety of ways. Given the limited numbers and capabilities of Soviet bombers, however, the United States has chosen not to develop a significant anti-aircraft defense network.

In marked contrast, the Soviet Union maintains a dense air defense network of surveillance radars, interceptor aircraft, and surface-to-air missiles aimed at destroying incoming U.S. bombers. However, the effectiveness of this system is questionable, given the vulnerability of air defenses to ballistic missile attack and the ability of low-flying aircraft and cruise missiles to evade detection.

Bomber lethality: Bombers are the slowest strategic delivery vehicles, taking eight to ten hours to reach enemy homelands. As a result, neither U.S. nor Soviet aircraft are capable of time-urgent missions against targets that must be destroyed quickly. American bombers are equipped with highly accurate weapons, however, and can "challenge the hardest of targets," according to the Joint Chiefs of Staff. Because of their maneuverability, moreover, they also can be used to attack mobile and imprecisely located targets.

Bomber survivability: Bombers are most vulnerable to attack on the ground, given the ease with which sprawling airfields can be targeted. As a result, roughly 30 percent of the U.S. bomber force is kept on "strip alert," ready to take off within moments after the launch of Soviet ICBMs is detected by U.S. warning systems. In contrast, few, if any, Soviet aircraft are kept on alert, leaving them highly susceptible to surprise attack.

The age of each bomber force also bears on its viability. Twenty-five-year-old Soviet aircraft have not been upgraded, although U.S. bombers—averaging 20 years in service—have been modernized repeatedly to ensure they are effective.

Traits of Bomber Forces

Both	**United States**	**Soviet Union**
Flexible	Highly capable	Minimal strategic
Slow		capabilities
Recallable	Old but upgraded	Old/not upgraded
Old	On alert	Not on alert
	(Minimal air defenses)	(Active air defenses)

In sum, U.S. strategic aircraft are far superior to their Soviet counterparts, providing a dimension to the American nuclear arsenal that is unmatched by the Soviet Union.

Land-based Ballistic Missiles

Intercontinental ballistic missiles (ICBMs) are a significant component of the American strategic triad, but are even more important to the Soviet Union, which is limited both in its access to oceans and in its mastery of sea-based missile technologies.

The United States has 1,049 land-based intercontinental ballistic missiles. This force consists of older Titans and Minuteman IIs and newer Minuteman IIIs. The ICBMs are armed with a total of 2,149 warheads, comprising 22 percent of all U.S. strategic weapons.

The Soviet Union has 1,398 land-based intercontinental ballistic missiles. This force consists of older SS-11s and -13s and newer SS-17s, -18s and -19s. The ICBMs are armed with a total of 5,862 warheads, comprising 73 percent of all Soviet strategic weapons.

Size of ICBM Forces

	United States	Soviet Union
ICBM launchers	1,049	1,398
ICBM warheads	2,149	5,862
(as percent of total warheads)	(22%)	(73%)

Several qualitative factors have an important bearing on the contribution of land-based missiles to the arsenals of the United States and the Soviet Union.

ICBM lethality: ICBMs, launched from stationary silos, currently are the most accurate ballistic missiles. Moreover, their flight time to enemy targets is as little as 30 minutes, making them suitable for time-urgent missions against enemy missile silos.

Until recently, the Soviet Union lacked the technological expertise necessary to achieve missile accuracies comparable to those of the United States. It compensated for this disadvantage in precision by designing larger missiles capable of carrying warheads with greater explosive power.

During the past decade, both the United States and the Soviet Union have made marked improvements in weapon precision. Today some modern U.S. and Soviet ICBMs can land within 600 to 800 feet, respectively, of their targets.

ICBM survivability: Currently, all U.S. and Soviet ICBMs are housed in stationary underground silos that are *hardened* with concrete to withstand pressure from a nuclear explosion. Despite these measures, recent improvements in weapon accuracy pose a threat to both nations' ICBMs and promise to overwhelm further efforts to "superharden" silos. As a result, the United States and the Soviet Union face the increasing vulnerability of their land-based weapons in fixed locations.

In theory, this problem is worse for the U.S. ICBM force because of the greater number of ICBM warheads that the Soviet Union can target against U.S. missile silos (a ratio of five to one). Some observers claim that the large numbers, high accuracy, and powerful yield of Soviet weapons could threaten the survivability of the entire U.S. ICBM force and increase the risk of a Soviet first strike. This controversial claim is examined under a subsequent heading, "Comparing First-Strike Capabilities."

ICBM penetrability: In general, ballistic missiles are assured of penetrating enemy territory. In the words of retired Admiral Noel Gayler, "Effective defense against hundreds or thousands of weapons is impossible."

Moreover, the use of defensive measures against ballistic missiles currently is constrained by international agreement. In 1972, the United States and the Soviet Union signed a treaty to limit *anti-ballistic missiles (ABMs)*—weapons intended to locate and destroy incoming warheads. The terms of the original treaty permitted each nation to maintain two ABM sites, but subsequent agreement reduced that number to one apiece. Since then, the United States has elected to dismantle its site near North Dakota missile fields. The Soviet Union still maintains a minimal site around its capital, "but this system is believed to be incapable of defending Moscow from even small-scale attacks," states a report prepared by a panel of strategic experts for the Carnegie Endowment for International Peace.

ICBM controllability: According to the Joint Chiefs of Staff, U.S. ICBMs have been upgraded over the years to provide "redundant and secure communications" with national command authorities and to improve their alert rates, or readiness, in case of attack. As a result, our ICBMs are capable of responding to command within minutes. Although the Soviet ICBM force also can be brought to alert quickly, the level of readiness appears to be somewhat lower in the Soviet Union—a fact attributed in part to the Soviet tradition of strict centralized command and reluctance to delegate authority.

Traits of ICBM Forces

Both	United States	Soviet Union
Accurate	Edge in accuracy	Lead in power
Prompt	(No ABM system)	(Ineffective ABM
Vulnerable		system)
Responsive		

In sum, the United States and the Soviet Union are reasonably matched in the critical qualitative elements—accuracy and yield—of their land-based missiles. Both forces currently represent potent threats to enemy missile silos.

Submarine-launched Ballistic Missiles

Submarine-launched ballistic missiles (SLBMs) are a key component of both U.S. and Soviet nuclear arsenals. However, American advantages in naval capabilities and technologies are reflected in the size and quality of the U.S. SLBM force.

Quantitative Comparisons

The United States has 520 sea-based ballistic missiles on submarines. The force consists of older Poseidon C-3s and newer Trident I C-4s. The SLBMs are armed with a total of 4,800 warheads, comprising 50 percent of all U.S. strategic weapons.

The Soviet Union has 969 ballistic missiles on submarines. This force consists of older SS-N-5s and SS-N-6s, and newer SS-N-8s, SS-N-17s and SS-N-18s. These SLBMs are armed with a total of 1,865 warheads, comprising 23 percent of all Soviet strategic weapons.

Size of SLBM Forces

	United States	Soviet Union
SLBM launchers	520	969
SLBM warheads	4,800	1,865
(as percent of total warheads)	(50%)	(23%)

Several qualitative factors influence the contribution of SLBMs to the arsenals of the United States and the Soviet Union.

SLBM survivability: Submarine-launched ballistic missiles, when on station at sea, are the most survivable of all strategic systems. Carried by submerged, constantly moving submarines and protected by vast ocean space, SLBMs are virtually impossible to target. Experts predict this invulnerability will continue for the foreseeable future, at least through the end of the century.

The survivability of SLBMs is assured by the number of submarines that are on patrol, rather than in port. The United States keeps over 50 percent of its force at sea, while the Soviet Union, constrained by maintenance and servicing problems, deploys only 15 to 20 percent of its submarines at any one time. Moreover, U.S. submarines are quieter than their Soviet counterparts, and thus are harder to detect and attack.

Sophisticated detection and tracking equipment, coupled with favorable geography, offers the United States a lead in *anti-submarine warfare (ASW)*—operations for locating, tracking, and destroying enemy submarines. By contrast, defense specialist John Collins asserts that the Soviet Union has "no way to impose ASW barriers between U.S. bases and open water. Searching for our submarines on station is like looking for a needle in a haystack." Given these factors, American submarine-launched missiles currently are regarded as the most invulnerable leg of the nuclear triad.

SLBM lethality: The accuracy of sea-based missiles is limited by the fact that they are launched from submerged, constantly moving submarines. Although targeting accuracies have improved in recent years, SLBM warheads still lack the combination of precision and yield necessary to destroy enemy missile silos. The United States continues to lead the Soviet Union in guidance technology, however, and our currently deployed Trident I missiles are capable of destroying most kinds of military installations.

SLBM penetrability: U.S. and Soviet sea-launched missiles, like their land-based counterparts, are virtually assured of penetrating enemy territory. Neither country currently has an effective anti-ballistic missile defense.

SLBM controllability: Shore-to-ship transmissions are difficult between national authorities and fast-moving submarines submerged in distant ocean patrol areas. Communication problems could be exacerbated during war, when radio contact would be subject to time delays and more vulnerable to detection and interruption.

Traits of SLBM Forces

Both	United States	Soviet Union
Invulnerable	Quiet subs	Noisy subs
Short flight time	Better technology/ accuracy	
Risky communi- cations		
	(Better ASW)	(Limited ASW)
	(No ABM)	(Ineffective ABM)

In sum, American submarine-launched missiles are more advanced and protected than their Soviet counterparts, providing the United States with a formidable strategic force at sea.

Comparisons of the kinds of weapons comprising U.S. and Soviet nuclear forces suggest that the balance of nuclear forces is in fact a "balance of imbalances": Soviet forces are stronger in some respects, U.S. forces are stronger in others, but overall the two are roughly equal. Harold Brown, Secretary of Defense in the Carter Administration, offers this assessment:

> In the first place, because nuclear weapons are so catastrophically damaging, small differences matter little. The balance is not made precarious because the other side has advantages by some measures. The risk would be greater if such advantages created, or were distorted into, the perception of being ahead across the board. The risk would be severe if there arose any doubt in our own minds or in those of our friends about our ability or our will to retaliate under any and all circumstances. The Soviets do not have, in my judgment, anything like strategic superiority in the sense of a militarily or politically usable advantage in strategic nuclear forces. They do have some advantages in the balance, but the United States also has some.

In a similar vein, Leslie Gelb, Director of the State Department's Bureau of Politico-Military Affairs during the Carter Administration, writes:

> The experts who look at all of these factors call the strategic balance a draw. Put another way, I have yet to meet a senior American military officer involved in this subject who would trade the American arsenal for the Soviet one. Only those experts who focus exclusively on Soviet superiority in land-based missiles think otherwise. And here the debate among the experts ascends to the level of theology.

The theology referred to by Gelb generally arises from comparisons of U.S. and Soviet *force exchanges*—mathematical predictions of how U.S. and Soviet arsenals would interact in the event of nuclear war. These calculations, based on hypothetical first-strike scenarios, offer a dynamic view of the strategic balance.

Comparing First-Strike Capabilities

Comparisons of force exchanges examine the relative outcomes of nuclear attacks on the U.S. and Soviet Union. Based on pencil-and-paper calculations and simulated computer games, the comparisons commonly measure the effects of counterforce strikes on enemy military targets. Such analyses reveal whether any advantage can be gained from "going first" in a crisis, even when forces are basically equivalent.

Assume, for example, that two opposing nuclear nations have comparable capabilities: each side's arsenal has three missiles, and each missile is armed with six warheads.

Nuclear Arsenal	Country A	Country B
Total missiles	3	3
Warheads per missile	6	6

Using the standard "rule of thumb" for targeting*—two warheads per target to ensure its destruction—if Country A were to strike first in this situation, its use of just one missile would enable it to destroy all three of Country B's missiles while still retaining two missiles of its own in reserve.

In the context of current U.S. and Soviet nuclear arsenals, such a *disarming first strike*—one that destroys most or all of the enemy forces before they can be launched—is impossible. Both sides have substantial nuclear forces that could survive and retaliate against the aggressor. However, some military strategists fear that current disparities in land-based missiles might be exploited by the Soviets in a limited first strike against U.S. silos.

This problem, popularly termed the *window of vulnerability,* is an example of the kind of analysis produced by simulated force exchanges. According to this scenario, the Soviet Union could use just a portion of its large and powerful ICBM force to destroy over 90 percent of U.S. ICBMs, as well as some U.S. bombers and submarines in port. The strike would leave the United States largely dependent on its submarine-based missiles—forces lacking the accuracy to destroy remaining Soviet ICBMs in their silos. Under these circumstances, some strategists claim, a U.S. president would be faced with the choice of either (1) attacking soft Soviet targets such as cities, thus inviting a Soviet counterattack on American cities, or (2) doing nothing and acceding to Moscow's political demands.

This scenario, according to other experts, is based on several unstated and dubious assumptions. First, a Soviet leader would have to be confident of his forces' ability to carry out a technically perfect attack, despite their lack of experience in such a large-scale and unprecedented mission. For example, the range over which most Russian missiles are tested is far shorter than the distance they would travel in wartime. Second, he would have to assume that the United States would not decide to launch on warning, firing off U.S. missiles before Soviet warheads arrived. Third, the Soviet leader would have to be convinced that an American president

---

*This standard formula is based on the assumption that an attacker probably would not risk a first strike without two warheads for each target, to allow for malfunctioning, hardened targets or errors in accuracy.

would choose to do nothing rather than retaliate, despite the enormous devastation that the United States would have suffered in a counterforce attack.

Moreover, such a scenario ignores certain U.S. military capabilities designed to deter such a strike. Even in the event of attack, the United States would have ample submarine forces to destroy soft but crucial military targets, such as Soviet airfields, submarine bases, and other installations. Moreover, the United States could draw upon the slow but hard-target capabilities of its alert bomber force to destroy Soviet silos. As former Defense Secretary Brown notes:

> The only thing missing from this scenario is the capability to hit their strategic ICBMs within a half hour instead of 10 hours. I submit this is not a central issue in the midst of a thermonuclear war.

Given these constraints, it is equally implausible that American leaders would launch a first strike against the Soviet Union. As Jerome Wiesner, Special Assistant for Science and Technology to President Kennedy, notes, ". . . by the same logic, the Soviet Union would certainly retain the capacity to inflict unacceptable punishment on the United States, no matter how large and clever a surprise first strike the U.S. were to launch." Accordingly, Dr. Wiesner concludes in a 1982 article in *The Atlantic Monthly:*

> At the moment, neither the U.S. nor the Soviet Union has a meaningful strategic advantage. A window of vulnerability does not exist. Furthermore, it is almost impossible to imagine how either side could achieve a usable advantage. Both sides are thoroughly deterred from using their strategic forces, because a decision to use them would be a decision to commit national suicide.

■ On Balance

Several conclusions may be drawn from this survey of U.S. and Soviet strategic capabilities. On balance, the American nuclear arsenal is equal if not superior to its Soviet counterpart. Moreover, the so-called window of vulnerability does not exist, chiefly because the United States has multiple forces that collectively guarantee retaliation—a fact recognized by President Reagan's Commission on Strategic Forces. Finally, both the United States and the Soviet Union, as currently armed, face a reciprocal threat of destruction in the event of nuclear war. Writing in 1956, President Dwight Eisenhower anticipated the day when the use of nuclear weapons would spell mutual disaster for both superpowers. At that point, he explained:

> . . . arguments as to the exact amount of available strength as compared to somebody else's are no longer the vital issues. When we get to [that] point . . . possibly we will have sense enough to meet at the conference table with the understanding that the era of armaments has ended and the human race must conform its actions to this truth or die.

■ Selected Sources

Robert P. Berman and John C. Baker, *Soviet Strategic Forces: Requirements and Responses* (The Brookings Institution, 1982).

Matthew Bunn and Kosta Tsipis, "The Uncertainties of a Preemptive Nuclear Attack," *Scientific American,* November 1983.

Carnegie Panel on U.S. Security and the Future of Arms Control, *Challenges for U.S. National Security: A Preliminary Report* (Carnegie Endowment for International Peace, 1981).

John M. Collins, *U.S.-Soviet Military Balance: Concepts and Capabilities 1960-1980* (McGraw-Hill, 1980).

———, *U.S./Soviet Military Balance: Statistical Trends, 1970-1982* (Congressional Research Service, The Library of Congress, October 1981/updated August 1983).

Thomas B. Cochran, William M. Arkin, and Milton M. Hoenig, *Nuclear Weapons Databook: U.S. Nuclear Forces and Capabilities* (Natural Resources Defense Council, Inc., 1984)

Department of Defense, *Soviet Military Power 1983* (Government Printing Office, 1983).

Leslie H. Gelb, "Nuclear Bargaining: The President's Options," *The New York Times Magazine,* June 27, 1982.

The International Institute for Strategic Studies, *The Military Balance 1982-1983* (The International Institute for Strategic Studies, 1982).

Joint Chiefs of Staff, *United States Military Posture for FY 1983* (Government Printing Office, 1983).

Fred Kaplan, "Missile Envy," *The New Republic,* October 11, 1982.

Teena Mayers, *Understanding Nuclear Weapons and Arms Control: A Guide to the Issues* (Arms Control Research, 1983).

Stockholm International Peace Research Institute, *The Arms Race and Arms Control* (Oelgeschlager, Gunn and Hain, Inc., 1982).

Jerome B. Wiesner, "Russian and American Capabilities," *The Atlantic Monthly,* July 1982.

III. HOW CAN NUCLEAR WAR BE PREVENTED?

The central problem of our time . . .
is how to employ human intelligence
for the salvation of mankind. It is a
problem we have put upon
ourselves.

General Omar Bradley
Former Chairman of the
Joint Chiefs of Staff
1957

Can Arms Control Help Prevent Nuclear War?

Upon reviewing the state of the nuclear balance, the wise observer is bound to ask not "Who's ahead?" but "What next?" The prospect of unrelenting arms competition invites exploration of different ways to manage nuclear rivalry in the future.

Public concern about nuclear war has spurred interest in cooperative rather than competitive paths to security. Former Secretary of State Cyrus Vance and former National Security Council staff member Robert Hunter explain this approach:

> The two superpowers—plus all other countries—are in the same boat and will survive or founder together. Neither the United States nor the Soviet Union can provide for its own security against nuclear holocaust unless it also helps to provide that security for the other.

Providing for common security, according to this view, depends on a policy of mutual restraint as well as mutual deterrence. Controlling the threat of war demands that the weapons themselves be controlled or regulated by international agreement.

To the public at large, however, nuclear arms control often is cast as either sin or salvation, an approach that impedes understanding and polarizes debate. Today, citizens must question the popular rhetoric and examine arms control policy on its merits.

■ The Need for Arms Control

Although the generic term *arms control* can be characterized in numerous ways, John Reichart and Steven Sturm offer a classic definition in their book, *American Defense Policy:*

> Arms control is usually understood to comprise all measures of regulating military forces by agreement; reductions of weapons; limitations on their number; restrictions on the deployment, exercise, or use of force; prohibition on research and development of a military character and related measures.

In this context, arms control incorporates all degrees of restricting weapons. The terms *arms limitation, arms reduc-*

tion, and *disarmament*—although often contrasted in popular usage and political rhetoric—are related concepts that denote different levels of arms control. In addition, arms control covers all kinds of agreement, from formal treaties to informal understandings between nations.

Common to all these approaches is the premise that national security is improved when we limit our armaments through diplomatic agreements that require our opponent to do the same. The notion that negotiated security may be preferable to rivalry is not new. It gained credence in this country as early as 1817, when the United States signed the Rush-Bagot Treaty with Great Britain to demilitarize the Great Lakes. Since then, arms control has been a variable but enduring feature of American security policy. In recent years, the development of nuclear weapons and the quickening pace of superpower rivalry have given new urgency to arms control—a fact attributable to the particular danger of the nuclear arms race.

The Danger of the Nuclear Arms Race

In an environment of uncontrolled competition, nuclear adversaries face the prospect of ever-changing weapons inventories. Unable to calculate or predict enemy capabilities, each nation constantly fears that its retaliatory forces may be rendered vulnerable over time. Similarly, each side worries that the balance of forces may shift unfavorably and confer some political or military advantage on its rival.

This mutual insecurity has several troubling implications for military planning and responses. It creates incentives for each side to develop new weapons based on "worst case" assumptions about the other side's plans. It creates pressures on each side to launch nuclear weapons first in a crisis. And it creates a climate in which overreaction and misjudgment by either side could trigger a nuclear exchange.

The need for nuclear arms control thus arises from the volatile nature of the arms race and the threat it poses to national security.

The Goal of Nuclear Arms Control

Traditionally, arms control efforts have been associated with three broad aims: reducing the likelihood of war, limiting the destructiveness of war if it occurs, and lessening the cost of preparing for war. Today, the growing danger of nuclear rivalry is prompting a preeminent focus on the first of these goals—preserving nuclear peace.

Current literature on arms control generally refers to two related aspects of nuclear peace: crisis stability and arms race stability. *Crisis stability* is present when neither party be-

---

A Chronology of Arms Control Efforts

Major Arms Control Agreements Signed and/or Ratified by the United States

The 1959 Antarctic Treaty demilitarizes the Antarctic. Signed by 23 nations.

The 1963 Limited Test Ban Treaty bans nuclear weapons tests in the atmosphere, in outer space, and under water. Signed by 109 nations.

The 1963 U.S.-Soviet Hot Line Agreement establishes a direct emergency communications link between the superpowers.

The 1967 Outer Space Treaty bans the placement of nuclear or any other weapons of mass destruction in outer space and the establishment of military bases, installations, or fortifications on the moon or other celestial bodies. Signed by 80 nations.

The 1967 Latin American Nuclear-Free Zone Treaty prohibits the testing, use, manufacture, production, or acquisition by any means of nuclear weapons in Latin America. Under Protocol II the nuclear weapons states agree to respect the military denuclearization of Latin America. Signed by 22 nations.

The 1968 Non-Proliferation Treaty (NPT) prohibits the transfer of nuclear weapons by states that have them and the acquisition of such weapons by those that do not and requires nuclear weapons states to seek nuclear disarma-*(continued)*

ment. Signed by 117 nations.

The 1971 Seabed Treaty bans the placement of weapons of mass destruction on the seabed beyond a 12-mile zone outside a nation's territory. Signed by 68 nations.

The 1971 U.S.-Soviet "Accidents Measures" Agreement pledges each party to guard against accidental or unauthorized use of nuclear weapons and provides for immediate notification of any accidental, unauthorized incident involving a possible detonation of a nuclear weapon.

The 1972 Biological Weapons Convention prohibits the development, production, stockpiling, or acquisition of biological agents and any weapons designed to use such agents. Signed by 90 nations.

The 1972 ABM Treaty and 1974 protocol limit U.S. and Soviet deployment of antiballistic missile defenses to a single site.

The 1972 Interim Offensive Weapons Agreement (technically expired on October 3, 1977, but is still observed) froze the number of U.S. and Soviet ballistic missile launchers for five years. (This agreement and the ABM Treaty are known as **SALT I**.)

The 1973 Agreement on the Prevention of Nuclear War provides that the United States and Soviet Union will make the removal of the danger of war and the use of nuclear weapons an objective of their policies, practice restraint in their relations toward each other and all countries, and pursue policies dedicated to peace and stability.

The 1974 Threshold Test Ban (TTB) Treaty limits U.S. and Soviet underground tests of nuclear weapons to 150 kilotons. Signed by both United States and Soviet Union but not ratified by U.S.

The 1976 Peaceful Nuclear Explosions (PNE) Treaty limits U.S. and Soviet underground nuclear explosions for peaceful purposes to 150 kilotons. Signed by both United States and Soviet Union but not ratified by U.S.

The 1977 Environmental Modification Convention prohibits the hostile use of techniques that could produce substantial environmental modifications. Signed by 32 nations.

The 1979 SALT II Treaty sets equal aggregate ceilings on a number of strategic nuclear systems, including the maximum number of strategic delivery vehicles (ICBMs, SLBMs, and intercontinental bombers), the maximum number of launchers of ballistic missiles with multiple warheads (MIRVs), and the maximum number of launchers of MIRVed ICBMs. The treaty also bans construction of additional, fixed ICBM launchers and a number of other improvements to existing weapons. Signed by both United States and Soviet Union but not ratified by U.S.

Recent Arms Control Negotiations

Mutual and Balanced Force Reductions (MBFR) Negotiations, multilateral talks seeking to limit NATO and Warsaw forces within a limited geographic region. Initiated in 1973. Negotiations in Vienna were recessed on December 15, 1983, and are scheduled to resume in mid-March, 1984.

Comprehensive Test Ban (CTB) Negotiations, talks among the United States, the Soviet Union, and Great Britain that seek to ban all nuclear weapons tests. Initiated in 1977. Negotiations in Geneva were adjourned indefinitely in 1980, and the Reagan Administration has not sought their resumption.

Anti-Satellite (ASAT) Weapons Negotiations, talks between the United States and Soviet Union on limiting the further development and deployment of anti-satellite weapons. Initiated in 1978. Negotiations in Geneva were adjourned indefinitely in 1979, and the Reagan Administration has not sought their resumption.

Intermediate-Range Nuclear Forces (INF) Negotiations, talks between the United States and Soviet Union on limiting intermediate-range nuclear forces in Europe. Initiated in 1981. Negotiations in Geneva were discontinued by the Soviet Union on November 23, 1983, following the arrival of new American missiles in West Germany and Great Britain.

Strategic Arms Reduction Talks (START), negotiations between the United States and Soviet Union on the reduction of strategic nuclear weapons (name changed from SALT to START). Initiated in 1982. Negotiations in Geneva were recessed on December 8, 1983, without the Soviet Union's agreeing to a date for their resumption.

—from *The Quest for Arms Control: Why and How,* prepared by the League of Women Voters Education Fund. Used by permission. •

lieves it has to use its nuclear weapons first during an international crisis; that is, each side can afford to wait without jeopardizing its ability to retaliate effectively. Whether a nation strikes first or is struck first has little bearing on the level of damage that each nation will sustain, given the magnitude of devastation in either case. *Arms race stability* exists when neither side feels it has to compete with the other in building up more or better nuclear weapons. Both sides are confident that mutual deterrence is ensured by their existing nuclear arsenals. Neither party believes that the development or deployment of additional weapons will confer any political or military advantage on itself or its adversary.

According to arms control theory, this kind of stalemate between the United States and the Soviet Union is preferable to endless "racing" and more readily achievable than global nuclear disarmament, an elusive long-term goal. Negotiated agreements thus hold out the promise of moderating competition in an environment shaped by the existence of nuclear weapons. As Leslie Gelb, Director of the State Department's Bureau of Politico-Military Affairs in the Carter Administration, explains:

> Without such negotiated mutual restraint, the competition would be far less controllable and both sides could acquire capabilities that just might make nuclear war more thinkable. It is not a way of solving our security problem. It is a way of preserving the Soviet-American "peace" that, with great good luck, has survived the last 40 years of tension and waste. To ask much more of a bargaining process between two powerful countries so mistrustful of each other is to condemn it to failure.

■ The Elements of Arms Control

Successful arms control demands that negotiators craft agreements serving the separate and shared interests of both parties involved. This mutually beneficial approach helps ensure that national security aims are furthered—that each nation perceives that it is better off with the agreement than without it. In principle, arms control provides an opportunity for the United States and the Soviet Union to serve their mutual interest in avoiding nuclear war.* The security of both nations can be enhanced by agreements that remove pressures to strike first, that increase the ability of each side to calculate and predict the military forces of the other, and that reduce the likelihood of nuclear escalation through mis-

---

*Soviet attitudes are discussed at length in Chapter 8, "Do the United States and the Soviet Union Have Mutual Interests?"

Limiting Numbers of Weapons: SALT, START, Build-Down

Quantitative curbs on the nuclear arms race have been a constant feature in the **Strategic Arms Limitation Talks (SALT)** between the United States and the Soviet Union. The first phase of negotiations—referred to as **SALT I**—was suggested by President Lyndon Johnson and launched by President Richard Nixon in 1969. These talks culminated with the signing of two documents in 1972, one of which—the **Interim Agreement**—offered temporary measures for restricting U.S. and Soviet nuclear weapons.

The Interim Agreement developed the basic concept of a "freeze" to guide the size of nuclear arsenals. Simply stated, a freeze tells nuclear nations, "Stop wherever you are," and fixes forces at existing levels. Based on this principle, the SALT I Agreement imposed a five-year moratorium on U.S. and Soviet launcher totals for land- and sea-based missiles. A further provision allowed each side to add a limited number of SLBMs so long as an equal number of older ICBMs and SLBMs were taken out of service. Since SALT I, numerous arms control proposals have been proposed and debated, each taking different "cuts" at the strategic balance.

The second phase of the Strategic Arms Limitation Talks—**SALT II**—was held for seven years under the administrations of Presidents Nixon, Ford, and Carter. Signed by President Carter and Soviet President Brezhnev in June 1979, the SALT II Treaty was withdrawn from Senate consideration in January 1980 following the Soviet invasion of Afghanistan. Upon assuming office, President Reagan decided not to resubmit the agreement for ratification. He pledged, however, to refrain from actions that would undercut SALT II "so long as the Soviet Union shows equal restraint."

The SALT II Treaty incorporates the principle of "numerical parity" as the standard for limiting nuclear weapons. Premised on the goal of "essential equivalence," the treaty specifies equal numerical ceilings for U.S. and Soviet weapons—an approach that tells the nuclear nations, "You can go this far, but no further." For example, the agreement sets an overall ceiling of 2,250 for total strategic launchers and limits the number of warheads that can be placed on various types of missiles. In effect, it puts a cap on existing levels of launchers and future levels of warheads.

In June 1982, the Reagan Administration reopened formal negotiations on long-range nuclear weapons, dubbing them **Strategic Arms Reduction Talks,** or **START.** The new title was chosen to signal a shift in emphasis from arms limitation to "deep cuts"—an approach that calls on the superpowers to reduce, rather than simply cap, their nuclear arsenals.

Despite the rhetoric of reductions, many observers have been troubled by the lack of progress in negotiations and the accelerated pace of the Administration's strategic modernization program. In response to this criticism—and in return for Congressional support for the proposed MX missile—President Reagan has announced his intention to broaden the U.S. negotiating plan, already revised several times, to incorporate the concept of a **build-down.** This new arms control initiative, promoted by Senators William Cohen (R-ME), Sam Nunn (D-GA), and others, calls for the retirement of old nuclear weapons as new ones are added to the arsenals of each superpower. Although the Senators' original formula tied the deployment of one warhead to the destruction of two older ones, the modified proposal outlines different "replacement ratios" for different types of missiles—an approach intended to discourage reliance on destabilizing weapons systems. For example, a country might have to withdraw two old land-based missile warheads for every new one added, but for less vulnerable submarine-based missiles the ratio would instead be a more favorable three to two. In sum, the build-down would permit the superpowers to upgrade the quality of their arsenals—and introduce more modern, lethal weapons—but only in return for net reductions in force levels. Whether these approaches would increase or decrease the stability of the nuclear balance is a hotly debated topic among arms control specialists.

On December 8, 1983, the latest round of the START negotiations recessed, and the Soviet Union—citing the new U.S. missile deployments in Europe—refused to set a date for the next session. ●

judgment. Negotiated agreements commonly incorporate several measures to accomplish these ends.

The Substance of Agreement

First, arms control agreements may specify *quantitative limits* on the size of nuclear arsenals. By limiting the numbers of nuclear weapons to prescribed levels, both American and Soviet leaders can calculate with greater certainty the size of the threat posed by enemy forces. Each nation is less likely to think that some numerical advantage can accrue to itself or its adversary. For example, the unratified SALT II Treaty limits both the United States and the Soviet Union to a maximum of ten warheads on each land-based missile. In the absence of that ceiling, the Soviet Union easily could increase the number of warheads on its large ICBMs, and pose an even greater threat to U.S. land-based forces. Moreover, reducing the size of nuclear arsenals is a direct, albeit gradual, step toward their ultimate elimination. "The way to get rid of nuclear weapons," observes retired Admiral Noel Gayler, "is to get rid of nuclear weapons."

Second, arms control agreements may specify *qualitative limits* on the kinds of weaponry in nuclear arsenals. This approach can enhance security by placing the tightest limits on those weapons that are most *destabilizing*. These include weapons that threaten either side's ability to retaliate, such as counterforce weapons or defensive systems, as well as weapons that are vulnerable to attack and thus compel nations to "use 'em or lose 'em" in a crisis. In addition, qualitative curbs can be imposed through bans on weapon testing. Such constraints can limit improvements in existing superpower arsenals as well as inhibit the spread, or *proliferation,* of nuclear weapons to other states.*

Third, arms control agreements may enumerate *verification measures* to assure each nation that the other is living up to the terms of agreement. These measures may include bans on active deception, guidelines for counting weapons, and agreed-upon procedures for data collection. Such mechanisms increase the visibility of adversary forces by helping provide accurate information on their size and composition. Moreover, they protect national security by deterring treaty violations that might upset the strategic balance.**

Finally, arms control agreements may include *confidence-building measures* to facilitate the prompt exchange of information between governments. For example, the United States and Soviet Union agreed in 1963 to establish an emer-

---

*The problem of proliferation is discussed in Chapter 8 under the heading, "Common Concern: Non-proliferation."

**Verification is discussed in Chapter 7, "Can the United States Verify Soviet Treaty Compliance?"

Limiting Kinds of Weapons: ABM Treaty, Test Bans, Nuclear Freeze

Qualitative curbs on the nuclear arms race have their roots in the landmark **ABM Treaty,** the second document produced by SALT I in 1972. In adopting the pact of unlimited duration, the United States and the Soviet Union singled out defensive weapons for constraint and agreed to limit the deployment of anti-ballistic missile systems to two areas—one for the defense of the national capital, and the other for the defense of ICBM fields. (Subsequent agreement restricted each nation to one deployment area.) According to *Time* diplomatic correspondent Strobe Talbott, these constraints reflected a basic premise that "in the games strategists play, the best offense is a good defense." Writing in 1979, he explained:

If one side is able to protect itself against the threat of a nuclear strike, that side is emboldened to throw its geopolitical weight around, and the other side is spurred to come up with new and better offensive weapons while at the same time improving its own defenses. ... The reciprocal self-denial of ABM in 1972 meant, to its American proponents, that each side was willingly exposing itself to the retaliatory deterrent of the other. Such mutual hostageship made it theo-
(continued)

retically inconceivable that either side would contemplate a preemptive strike. . . .

The notion that foregoing certain weaponry can enhance stability has been an enduring theme in the numerous test ban initiatives proposed and negotiated over the years.

The testing of explosive nuclear devices is considered essential to military confidence in new technology.* It helps facilitate the refinement of weapon design and ensure the workability of more deadly and efficient warheads. Curbing nuclear testing thus could have a powerful, inhibiting effect on the nuclear arms race. As McGeorge Bundy, Special Assistant for National Security Affairs to Presidents Kennedy and Johnson, observes:

We cannot stuff the thermonuclear genie all the way back in the jar, but if we can get both sides to stop *all* testing, even now, we can put an important brake on our still unbridled competition in nuclear technology.

Except for Ronald Reagan, every American president from the time of Eisenhower has pursued measures to limit nuclear weapons test explosions. The 1963 **Limited Test Ban Treaty** prohibits the testing of nuclear weapons in the atmosphere, underwater, and in outer space, but not underground. The 1974 **Threshold Test Ban Treaty**—still unratified— places a limit of 150 kilotons on the yield of any under-

*Confidence in existing weaponry, known as *stockpile reliability,* is assured primarily by non-nuclear testing, including inspection and disassembly of weapon parts.

ground nuclear test. The 1976 **Peaceful Nuclear Explosions Treaty**—also unratified—extends the 150-kiloton limit to nuclear tests for peaceful purposes (e.g., mining and geological exploration).

Despite these partial measures, the goal of a comprehensive test ban on *all* nuclear explosive testing— first embraced by President Eisenhower—has remained elusive. In 1977, formal negotiations for a **Comprehensive Test Ban Treaty (CTB)** were renewed by the United States, Soviet Union, and Great Britain. By 1979, substantial agreement had been reached, but the CTB talks were deferred indefinitely by President Reagan when he assumed office in 1981.

The idea of a total ban on nuclear testing is also a key aspect of a proposal for a **bilateral nuclear weapons freeze.** Popularized by Randall Forsberg, Director of the Institute of Defense and Disarmament Studies, the concept of a nuclear freeze has received widespread support in Congress and local communities across the nation since 1980. In spring 1983, a freeze resolution passed the House of Representatives by a vote of 278 to 149 but later was defeated during the fall Senate session by a vote of 58 to 40.

As originally conceived, the nuclear freeze proposal calls for a bilateral agreement between the United States and the Soviet Union to halt the following specific activities:

• the production of fissionable material (uranium-235 and plutonium) for nuclear weapons;

• the fabrication, assembly, and testing of nuclear warheads;
• the testing, production, and deployment of missiles designed to deliver nuclear warheads; and
• the testing of new types of aircraft and the production and deployment of any additional aircraft designed primarily to deliver nuclear weapons.

This comprehensive moratorium is designed to preclude the production of new counterforce weaponry and create a "breathing space" for U.S. and Soviet negotiators so that progress in arms reduction can be made. As Randall Forsberg explains:

The idea is to stop the nuclear arms race quite literally, by stopping the development and production of all nuclear-weapons systems in the two countries. . . . It would terminate the technological arms race and shut down entirely this wasteful and dangerous form of human competition.   •

gency communications link, or *hotline*—a teleprinter system that proved valuable during the 1967 Arab-Israeli War when it was used to prevent possible misunderstanding of American fleet movements in the Mediterranean. More recently, legislative proposals to enhance the hotline and establish a permanent U.S.-Soviet center for crisis management were offered by Senator Sam Nunn (D-GA) and the late Senator Henry Jackson (D-WA). Improving channels of communication and consultation between the superpowers may ease the danger of miscalculation during times of international crisis.

All four types of restrictions on nuclear forces—quantitative and qualitative limits, verification, and confidence-building measures—thus have the potential to enhance the common security of the United States and the Soviet Union while accommodating each nation's separate interests.

The Process of Agreement

To design a mutually beneficial arrangement, the United States and the Soviet Union must engage in some form of bargaining. Traditionally, nuclear arms control has been dominated by a process of treaty negotiation, a framework that calls for explicit bargaining aimed at producing a written "contract" in the form of a treaty or executive agreement.* The formality of such proceedings is believed to foster several conditions that ease the risk of nuclear war.

First, treaties create international obligations that convey a sense of permanence and commitment to arms control. These conditions offer the superpowers a durable framework for comprehensive weapons restrictions, an approach that can enhance stability during periods of crisis.

Second, treaties define precisely the way to constrain adversarial weapons programs and to verify that both sides are keeping the bargain. Such precision may dampen superpower competition in several ways; for example, it removes pressures to build up forces based on "worst case" assumptions and introduces predictability into military planning.

Finally, the process of formal bargaining can have value independent of the agreement it produces. Treaty negotiations may help reduce hostility and enhance understanding between the United States and the Soviet Union by providing a forum for dialogue on matters of common interest.

These advantages notwithstanding, treaty negotiations also are characterized by their adversarial nature. Under the rubric of formal bargaining, each nation seeks to maximize its own

---

*According to U.S. law, an arms control agreement that is negotiated and signed by the president becomes legally binding on the United States only after the document meets with Congressional approval. To be ratified as a *treaty*, a signed pact must receive the consent of two-thirds of the Senate. In the alternative, it may be approved as an *executive agreement* by a simple majority of both houses of Congress.

Outpacing Arms Control: New Missiles in Europe

The "horse race" between arms control negotiations and changing force levels can be seen in Western Europe, where 572 new American intermediate-range missiles are being added to NATO's nuclear arsenal over the next five years. Currently, the United States has stationed in or around Europe roughly 6,000 assorted nuclear weapons, including battlefield weapons and weapons in nuclear-armed submarines and bombers. The scheduled deployments, now in progress, will give NATO two new land-based systems: American ground-launched cruise missiles and Pershing II ballistic missiles—highly accurate missiles that can strike Soviet territory within ten minutes of liftoff from some locations.

The decision to place these additional forces on European soil was made in 1979 by the United States and its NATO allies in response to the Soviets' modernization of their nuclear missiles aimed at Western Europe. This perceived challenge led NATO to explore steps that would demonstrate America's political commitment to European security and would counter the Soviet build-up of SS-20 missiles. A "two-track" policy emerged, calling for the placement of new American weapons in Europe while committing the United States to pursue negotiations with the Soviet Union to limit both sides' intermediate-range nuclear forces (INF).

position—an approach that can sustain and heighten arms competition in several ways.

First, the intractable problem of reaching consensus poses a dilemma for negotiators: in the quest for equal force levels, it typically is easier to get both parties to agree to common ceilings than to actual reductions in the size of their respective arsenals. Formal bargaining arguably fosters this tendency to level *up* to symmetry, a result criticized as "institutionalizing the arms race." For example, the 1974 Vladivostok accord, which was designed to set a framework for SALT II, provided limits of 2,400 for total strategic launchers and 1,320 for launchers with multiple warheads—ceilings that allowed the continued build-up of U.S. and Soviet nuclear forces.

A second controversial feature of arms control talks is the use of newly-developed weapons as "bargaining chips." This tactic, designed to induce the other side to negotiate seriously, may lead to building weapons systems that probably never would be deployed in the absence of negotiations. Once developed, however, such weapons become difficult to retire because of the political and bureaucratic support that grows for them. According to critics, weapons promoted as bargaining chips often end up as non-negotiable items, thwarting the arms control objective they originally were intended to serve. In 1972, for example, the development of the cruise missile was accelerated as a bargaining chip for SALT II, according to chief SALT I negotiator Gerard Smith. "Now, we have built hundreds of cruise missiles—and plan thousands more—and soon the Soviet Union will begin to deploy similar weapons," notes Smith in his 1983 article, "Chips Are No Bargain."

Third, formal arms control negotiations may involve protracted bargaining over a period of years; for example, the SALT I negotiations took four years; SALT II, seven. This lengthy process may be outpaced by changes in deployment levels and weapons technology—a result that can undermine the effectiveness of negotiations in progress while maintaining an illusion of security. Moreover, arms control treaties, according to some critics, may implicitly sanction the "technological arms race" and allow competition to flourish in areas not formally restricted by agreement. For example, the United States, having pioneered multiple warhead technology, was reluctant to negotiate a ban on MIRVs during SALT I. At the start of negotiations, the MIRV system was in the later stages of development; by the time the SALT agreement was reached, it was ready for full-scale deployment. The Soviet Union quickly matched the United States in MIRV technology, opening a veritable "Pandora's box" in nuclear weapons competition.

Finally, the specificity of treaty language may create incentives for nations to find loopholes that can be exploited to their own advantage. As explained by Leslie Gelb:

It is sometimes easier to behave sensibly than to contractualize a sensible arrangement . . . . U.S. negotiators are almost invariably given instructions, in effect, to close all the other side's loopholes but to keep their own open. Not surprisingly, Soviet instructions seem similar.

The need for nuclear rivals to "behave sensibly" is leading some specialists to advocate less rigid approaches to arms control. These include informal understandings and reciprocal "If you'll do it, I'll do it" restraints that rely on implicit bargaining to facilitate agreement. Interestingly, the first concrete step towards nuclear arms control embodied this informal approach. From 1958 to 1961, the United States and the Soviet Union observed a moratorium on nuclear testing based on matched but unilateral public statements. Similarly, the two nations pledged in 1963 to refrain from placing nuclear weapons in orbit—declarations that resulted in the 1967 Outer Space Treaty. These kinds of parallel actions—undertaken simultaneously or conditioned on reciprocity—provide mechanisms for restraint without the problems of detailed, prolonged negotiations.

There are, to be sure, certain drawbacks to informal arms control. Lacking the force of law, such measures may be less durable during times of crisis; lacking the precision of treaties, they may pose problems for verification. Like treaties, however, informal initiatives are likely to be honored as long as they remain mutually beneficial to participating nations.

Ultimately, durable efforts to restrain the nuclear arms race—whatever the framework for U.S.-Soviet agreement—must serve the separate and shared interests of the superpowers. They must, in the words of retired Admiral Noel Gayler, "remove our joint peril and enhance the security of both." This simple directive provides citizens and policymakers a valuable measuring rod against which future arms control initiatives can be assessed.

The INF negotiations between the United States and Soviet Union began in Geneva in November 1981. After two years of little progress, the talks have broken down as American missiles have begun to arrive in Europe. The Soviets' decision to suspend negotiations has been accompanied by threats to end their moratorium on new SS-20 deployments, introduce longer-range battlefield nuclear weapons based in Eastern Europe, and increase their missile capabilities on submarines patrolling near U.S. shores. Many observers note that new deployments of nuclear weaponry are, once again, outpacing arms control—a prospect that could bode ill for political and nuclear stability in Europe. Writing in May 1983, *Washington Post* reporter Walter Pincus cautioned:

Anti-nuclear groups in Western Europe, fired up by talk of an impending nuclear war, have mobilized millions of men, women and children for demonstrations and marches; Soviet officials are making public and private threats to deploy new nuclear weapons; West European governments and party coalitions face serious political challenges; even the future of the 34-year-old NATO alliance is said to be in jeopardy.

Thus . . . it seems the superpowers have voluntarily begun a game of nuclear "chicken" with the world looking on to see which one blinks first. •

■ Selected Sources

Arms Control Association, *Arms Control and National Security: An Introduction* (Arms Control Association, 1983).

"Arms, Defense Policy, and Arms Control," *Daedalus: Arms, Defense Policy, and Arms Control* (Journal of the American Academy of Arts and Sciences, Summer 1975).

Randall Forsberg, "A Bilateral Nuclear-Weapon Freeze," *Scientific American,* November 1982.

Noel Gayler, "How to Break the Momentum of the Nuclear Arms Race," *The New York Times Magazine,* April 25, 1982.

Leslie H. Gelb, "A Practical Way to Arms Control," *The New York Times Magazine,* June 5, 1983.

Jerome H. Kahan, "Arms Interaction and Arms Control," in *American Defense Policy,* edited by John F. Reichart and Steven R. Sturm (The Johns Hopkins University Press, 1982).

William H. Kincade and Jeffrey D. Porro, eds., *Negotiating Security: An Arms Control Reader* (The Carnegie Endowment for International Peace, 1979).

League of Women Voters, *The Quest for Arms Control: Why and How* (League of Women Voters Education Fund, 1983).

Alan Neidle, ed., *Nuclear Negotiations: Reassessing Arms Control Goals in U.S.-Soviet Relations* (University of Texas at Austin, 1982).

Gerard C. Smith, "Chips Are No Bargain," *The New York Times,* May 23, 1983.

———, *Doubletalk: The Story of the First Strategic Arms Limitation Talks* (Doubleday and Company, 1980).

Strobe Talbott, *Endgame: The Inside Story of SALT II* (Harper and Row, Publishers, Inc., 1979).

Cyrus R. Vance and Robert E. Hunter, "The Centrality of Arms Control," *The New York Times,* December 26, 1982.

Herbert F. York, "Bilateral Negotiations and the Arms Race," *Scientific American,* October 1983.

Any discussion of arms control turns inevitably to the issue of weapons innovation. The promise of new technology has been, and continues to be, a key force in nuclear arms competition and a major factor in the strategic balance.

Despite the appeal of a world with no nuclear arms, most observers are resigned to our coexistence with the hydrogen bomb, a product of mankind's inventiveness. As Lord Solly Zuckerman writes in *Nuclear Illusion and Reality,* "Nuclear weapons exist. The knowledge of how to make them exists, and cannot be made to vanish." Dr. Jerome Wiesner, Special Assistant for Science and Technology to President Kennedy, notes similarly, "The weapons that create the threat of annihilation cannot be uninvented."

Concern about the irreversible march of technology can heighten public skepticism of further inventions in nuclear weaponry. Yet the merits of innovation, to be fully explored and fairly debated, must be considered in the context of nuclear policy goals. What is the relationship of future technology to stability, to arms control, and to the ultimate goal of preventing nuclear war?

How Will New Technology Affect the Risk of Nuclear War?

■ Technology and Stability

Public comparisons of U.S. and Soviet weaponry commonly survey the current inventories of the superpowers. In assessing the strategic balance, however, policymakers also are attuned to the prospect of weapons innovation—the addition of some "new, improved" nuclear armament that could alter the balance of forces in the future.

Not surprisingly, the merits of weapons innovation are in the eye of the beholder. For the inventing nation, a new weapon may seem to remedy some perceived weakness or add some prized capability that bolsters its strength. For the other nation, however, it may create apprehension about the strategic balance, triggering defenses or countermeasures in response. Given these factors, most observers recognize the disquieting effect of technological change on nuclear stability. As explained by former Secretary of State and National Security Advisor Henry Kissinger, "Every country lives with the nightmare that even if it puts forth its best efforts its survival may be jeopardized by a technological breakthrough on the part of its opponent."

Such fears lead military planners to design their nuclear forces based on "technological anticipation," a phrase coined by arms control expert William Kincade. Simply stated, this means that each superpower assumes its own innovations are being matched by the enemy. The guiding premise is "whatever we can conceive, they will deploy," explains Kincade, his observation borne out by the experience of John Foster, Jr., Pentagon Director of Defense Research and Engineering from 1965 to 1973:

> Now most of the action the U.S. takes in the area of research and development has to do with one of two types of activities. Either we see from the fields of science and technology some new possibilities which we think we ought to exploit, or we see threats on the horizon, possible threats, usually not something the enemy has done, but something we have thought of ourselves that he might do, we must therefore be prepared for. These are the two forces that tend to drive our research and development activities.

Today, most policymakers agree that technological threats to the U.S. arsenal demand a careful response, yet they disagree on the *type* of response that will preserve nuclear stability and protect national interests. At the heart of this debate is the tension between new weapons technology and arms control—a seeming fork in the road in nuclear arms policy. Can solutions to the arms race be found on the technological frontier or do they lie in negotiations to limit superpower weaponry?

Forthcoming innovations in weapons technology promise to shape the direction of this policy debate. These include scientific developments affecting all aspects of Soviet and American nuclear forces, including their ability to destroy targets (lethality), their ability to survive surprise attack (survivability), their ability to penetrate enemy defenses (penetrability), and their ability to receive and respond to command (controllability).

■ Technology and Lethality

Several recent advances in warhead technology have increased each nation's confidence in the ability of its nuclear weapons to destroy enemy targets. During the past decade, there have been gradual but steady improvements in the accuracy of *inertial guidance systems,* the preprogrammed "brains" of ballistic missiles that detect and correct deviations from the weapon's intended course and speed. Today, a single warhead from a modern land-based missile has much better than a 50-50 chance of destroying an enemy silo or other hardened target. If two warheads are targeted on the silo, the probability of its destruction can be 90 percent or higher. Future refinements in inertial guidance systems will reduce ICBM delivery error even further, virtually assuring destruction of each hardened target by a single warhead.

These improvements in inertial guidance systems are being matched or even surpassed by other advances in guidance technology. *Stellar guidance systems* allow modern submarine-launched missiles to fix their locations against the stars and achieve virtually the same accuracy as ICBMs. *Terminal guidance systems,* designed to "read" and follow the terrain on approach to the target, are currently being used with cruise missiles; a similar scene-matching guidance system also is employed by the Pershing II missile and could be adapted to other ballistic missiles to advance their accuracy even further. New *navigation satellites,* in orbit to guide ships, airplanes, ground vehicles and submarines, could serve as future points of reference for land- and submarine-based missiles. Alternatively, hundreds of *ground beacons* could provide guidance to SLBMs or ICBMs from any position within line of sight. Each of these different technical paths will be available by the end of the decade—a prospect that has led many observers to dub this "the era of absolute accuracy."

Paralleling these developments in warhead guidance are steady advances in *re-entry and propulsion technology,* enabling the superpowers to put more warheads on each missile. Currently, the United States and the Soviet Union are tacitly abiding by the terms of the unratified SALT II Treaty, which limits their largest land-based missiles to ten warheads apiece. In the absence of SALT or other progress in arms control, both nations could increase this number by improving warhead or missile design or by using smaller, lower-yield warheads.

The advances in warhead precision, coupled with the increasing number of warheads per target, have ushered in an era when all fixed targets—even heavily protected missile silos—are highly vulnerable to attack. Most observers concur that this development has dramatic implications for nuclear stability. In a crisis, the "silo-busting" potential of modern weapons could increase incentives for a first strike—by either an attacker *or* an intended victim that fears the loss of its retaliatory capability. As a result of this threat, much technical planning in the United States is driven by the problem of assuring the survivability of our nuclear forces.

■ Technology and Survivability

It is frequently asserted that a triad of air, sea, and land weapons reinforces nuclear survivability in several ways:

- The existence of three legs requires the Soviets to diversify their research and development efforts, and also provides a hedge against possible Soviet breakthroughs in a single area.
- The existence of three legs complicates Soviet planning for a nuclear attack; for example, the launching of Soviet land-based missiles against U.S. ICBMs would provide enough warning time for our bomber force to take off; conversely, an early attack on our bomber bases by Soviet SLBMs would alert our land-based missiles before they could be struck by incoming ICBMs.
- Each leg has unique traits that are suitable for specific missions; for example, ICBMs are highly accurate and readily retargetable, while SLBMs are more secure, and bombers can be recalled or reused.

Some strategists claim that *each* of the triad's components must be survivable to protect national security. Many others maintain that the purpose of multiple forces is not to have complete survivability of all three legs but rather, by having three, to assure that one or two remain survivable. This latter perspective is endorsed by the President's Commission on Strategic Forces, a panel of former government and military officials chaired by retired Air Force General Brent Scowcroft:

> . . . the different components of our strategic forces should be assessed collectively and not in isolation . . . [Whereas] it is highly desirable that a component of the strategic forces be survivable when it is viewed separately, it makes a major contribution to deterrence even if its survivability depends in substantial measure on the existence of one of the other components of the force.

The problem of weapon system vulnerability thus may be overrated in policy planning. It is, nonetheless, a common rationale for developing new generations of weapons and, as such, demands thorough public understanding.

Land-based Missiles

The challenge in protecting land-based missiles is to secure the weapons at their launching position so that they can ride out a surprise attack. The destructive capabilities of modern warheads have led U.S. planners to explore different paths to reduce ICBM vulnerability.

One technical approach to the problem involves *super-hardening* missile silos to improve their resistance to the shock of nuclear explosions. Many observers maintain, however, that such attempts can be overwhelmed by improvements in warhead accuracy currently within the state of the art.

The inevitable vulnerability of fixed missile sites has directed technicians to a second approach: basing ICBMs in a way that would complicate Soviet attack plans. Several schemes aimed at confusing Soviet targeters involve mobile launchers that are moved over large areas of land among *multiple protective shelters*. This strategy would create a "shell game" for the attacker, requiring the Soviets to expend excess warheads to destroy fewer American missiles.

Alternatives to road mobile schemes include proposals to use aircraft-launched ICBMs, to base missiles in orbit, or to deploy ICBMs on small, offshore submarines. Yet another approach, promoted by the Reagan Administration in 1983, called for *closely-spaced basing*—bunching missile sites together in a "dense pack," so that early-arriving Soviet warheads would destroy or deflect the latecomers.

Although the various basing modes could be adapted to most ICBMs, these proposals generally have been considered in the context of a new land-based weapon system—the *Missile Experimental,* or *MX,* currently the subject of debate in Congress.

The MX is a large missile, capable of delivering ten or more nuclear warheads, each at least as precise and powerful as those of its predecessor, the improved Minuteman III. These traits provide the MX with a superior capacity as a "silo-buster," a fact that increases the threat posed to Soviet missile silos. Nonetheless, the MX was mainly touted, at least until recently, as a way to solve the problem of ICBM vulnerability rather than to enhance American counterforce potential.

During the past decade, more than 30 schemes for basing the MX have been devised and debated, yet none has garnered broad support from technical experts or politicians. This fruitless search has led many observers to question the advantage of the MX over the existing Minuteman missile system in terms of its survivability. Moreover, the ten-warhead MX missile may pose a more tempting target than the three-warhead Minuteman,* creating an "invitation to nuclear war," warns Dr. Herbert Scoville, Jr., former Deputy Director for Science and Technology at the Central Intelligence Agency.

Yet another plan calls for the development of a small, one-warhead *Midgetman missile,* a system accurate enough to destroy hard targets and deployable in both fixed and mobile basing modes. Instead of concentrating many warheads on a

---

*Using the targeting rule of thumb—two warheads per missile silo—Soviet war planners theoretically could attack an MX silo and use just two of their . warheads to destroy ten of ours. Against a Minuteman silo, two Soviet warheads would destroy only three of ours, a less favorable "exchange ratio" from the Soviet perspective.

The Scowcroft Report: A Confusing Package?

The debate about the MX missile is being shaped, in large measure, by the findings of the President's Commission on Strategic Forces. The commission—chaired by retired Air Force General Brent Scowcroft—was assembled by President Reagan in January 1983 to review the U.S. strategic program. Its report, issued in April 1983, included such recommendations as:

- an endorsement of the President's plan to deploy 100 MX missiles in existing Minuteman silos;
- a proposal to develop a mobile single-warhead missile that would be deployed in the early 1990s; and
- a suggestion that arms control agreements limit the number and size of warheads rather than launchers.

According to the commission's reasoning, the deployment of the MX—even in an admittedly vulnerable basing mode—would induce the Soviet Union to accept new arms control limits and to shift its forces, along with the United States, to a more stable structure of single-warhead missiles.

To many observers, however, the deployment of a multi-warhead MX missile in conjunction with the development of a one-warhead Midgetman is a self-contradictory *and* self-defeating package. Although the Commission

few large MIRVed missiles, dispersing them among many Midgetmen would reduce the value of each missile site to Soviet targeters and deplete the Soviet stockpile more quickly in the event of an attack.* Thus, the advent of a single-warhead missile system might remove incentives for a first strike and signal a trend toward "deMIRVing" nuclear forces—developments that could help "to ensure strategic stability amid the revolution wrought by thousands of warheads on only hundreds of launchers," writes Henry Kissinger. On the other hand, it could be a very costly system, and it might introduce verification problems that would complicate future arms control negotiations.

A third possible solution to ICBM vulnerability involves modernization of our submarine force, a step designed to reduce reliance on land-based missiles. To date, efforts in this area have centered on the development of a new generation of SLBMs—*Trident II (D5)* missiles—with longer ranges and the accuracy and power of modern land-based weapons. As with the MX, however, the usefulness of a silo-busting submarine missile is open to debate. William Perry, Under Secretary of Defense for Research and Engineering in the Carter Administration, explains:

> If you're going to be, in a sense, depending on subs for primary deterrence, what do you do that minimizes the attractiveness of the surprise attack? If I were the Soviet planner, I would be deterred from acting even by Trident I . . . .

Yet another possible solution to ICBM vulnerability lies not with offensive systems but with defensive ones, currently prohibited by the ABM Treaty. This fifth approach calls for protecting ICBMS at their bases with *ballistic missile defenses (BMDs),** a phrase describing systems that can locate and destroy incoming missiles or warheads. Unlike technology designed for area defense of cities—considered unworkable by many strategists and scientists—current BMD concepts are being explored to provide a point defense for missile silos and other critical targets, such as command and control facilities. In theory, such protective measures could decrease confidence in the effectiveness of a first strike; in practice, however, missile defense could have the opposite effect. A panel of Harvard University scholars offer this explanation in their book, *Living With Nuclear Weapons:*

---

*Against a Midgetman missile site, the Soviet Union would have to use two warheads to destroy only one of ours, an unfavorable exchange ratio for the Soviets.

**The term *anti-ballistic missile system (ABM)* often is used interchangeably with ballistic missile defense.

ABM technology has advanced over the past decade, but so has the offensive missile technology it is intended to counter, and the advantage remains with the offense . . . [I]f the Soviet Union developed a workable defensive system before the United States, for example, American officials would fear that Soviet incentives to avoid nuclear war would be diminished. A defense-dominated world might also be less stable depending on how perfect defense systems were believed to be. In such a world, there might be heightened incentives for surprise attack, or for efforts to develop new, more decisive offensive systems.

The problem of finding a technical "fix" to the ICBM vulnerability issue is prompting many legislators to call for new initiatives in the area of arms control. Some legislators see arms control as obviating the need for new weapons systems. For example, Representative Thomas Downey (D-NY) maintains that prohibitions on missile testing provided in the proposed nuclear weapons freeze, if adopted, would reduce Soviet confidence in the reliability of their MIRVed missiles and preclude Soviet advances in countersilo weapons. Other legislators, however, believe that a combination of arms control and new weapons systems would best address the problem of ICBM vulnerability. For example, Representative Albert Gore, Jr. (D-TN), an advocate of the Midgetman missile, recommends several measures—including reductions in warheads and restrictions on MIRVed missiles—to alleviate the disproportion between warheads and missile launchers.

Today, many government officials acknowledge the merits of a U.S.-Soviet agreement that would lead, eventually, to deMIRVing land-based missiles on both sides. Ironically, some policymakers also are prepared to endorse production of the ten-warhead MX missile, despite the inconsistency of these positions. Whatever the ultimate outcome of the MX debate, concern about ICBM vulnerability has prompted greater public scrutiny of the other legs of the triad and their prospects for survival in the future.

Submarines

Submarines are widely regarded as the most secure leg of the nuclear triad. In its recent report, the President's Commission on Strategic Forces confirmed this view:

The problem of conducting open-ocean search for submarines is likely to continue to be sufficiently difficult that ballistic missile submarine forces will have a high degree of survivability for a long time.

Despite such confidence, a few policymakers express concern about the prospects for improvements in *anti-*

espoused stability as its primary objective, it went in exactly the opposite direction by placing the lethal MX in vulnerable silos: "If there was ever a 'use it or lose it' system, ill-designed for stability in a crisis, it is this one," writes McGeorge Bundy, Special Assistant for National Security Affairs to Presidents Kennedy and Johnson. Moreover, the supposed rationale for the MX—to pressure the Soviets at the bargaining table—is flawed, according to Bundy and others. He explains:

The Soviet answer to new programs will be new programs, not new concessions. If the commission wants a no-new MIRV agreement, which would make good sense, it should propose just that. It should not pretend that the MX in Minuteman silos is arms control in disguise . . . . In spite of the commission's unexplained insistence that all its ideas make a single package, Congress has every right and duty to take only what it finds truly needed. •

submarine warfare against nuclear-armed submarines. *Strategic ASW,* as it is called, has three component parts. First, a submarine must be located and reliably tracked. Then it must be identified as an enemy submarine carrying nuclear missiles. Finally, it must be destroyed.

The difficult nature of each of these steps casts doubt on the effectiveness of anti-submarine warfare. Even if this complex mission could succeed against one strategic submarine, it is considered highly unlikely that ASW could destroy more than a fraction of a missile submarine fleet ranging the world's oceans. Moreover, there already exist several technologies that provide countermeasures to anti-submarine warfare. For example, the use of quiet-running electric submarines, jamming techniques, and noisy decoys can reduce the effectiveness of sound-detecting sensors relied on for ASW missions. As a result, even concentrated Soviet resources in ASW research pose an unlikely threat to American submarines: "The subject is not money-limited," explains William Nierenberg, Director of Scripps Oceanographic Institution.

Indeed, many observers suggest that technical improvements in anti-submarine warfare—a field led by the United States—pose a greater threat to Soviet missile submarines, given their confined access to oceans through narrow straits. As a result, strategies to restructure Soviet forces away from large, land-based systems to the sea will depend, in part, on Soviet confidence in the survivability of their submarines.

In light of these factors, proposals to curb ASW competition are receiving increasing attention in arms control literature. However, the need to develop ASW technology to protect naval vessels and vital sea lines of communications complicate efforts to constrain certain forms of ASW hardware and measures. There are no negotiations addressing these issues at present; nevertheless, many arms control specialists maintain that a timely agreement in this area could help limit the threat of anti-submarine warfare *before* new technology endangers the survivability of strategic submarines in the future.

Bombers

Maintaining the survivability of bombers poses a different set of challenges to military planners. Aircraft on the ground are highly vulnerable to destruction in the event of a nuclear attack. As a result, about 30 percent of the U.S. bomber force is kept on strip alert and can be airborne within minutes. However, missiles launched from enemy submarines patrolling along our coast would offer little warning time—less than twelve minutes for Soviet SLBMs at close range.

Most strategists acknowledge the unresolved technical problems faced by Soviet leaders in contemplating this type of attack. For example, an early assault on bomber bases would alert U.S. ICBM missile sites and allow those weapons to be launched. Nonetheless, concern about close-in submarines has prompted American technicians to develop changes in bomber design that will ensure faster takeoff from airstrips.

The *B-1 bomber* is designed to upgrade the U.S. B-52 force with certain features that enhance survivability. It is more resistant to nuclear weapons effects and able to escape its base more quickly. However, other characteristics of the B-1 bomber—discussed in the following pages—have drawbacks that call into question the viability of the proposed new aircraft. As a result, alternative approaches to improved bomber survivability are being advanced. For example, one arms control initiative, explored tentatively during SALT II, would prohibit U.S. and Soviet submarines from patrolling close to each other's shores, thus reducing the risk of a surprise attack on bomber bases.

Protecting strategic bombers also depends on the security of the aircraft once aloft and en route to target. In this context, the ability of bombers to penetrate enemy defenses is central to military confidence.

■ Technology and Penetrability

To carry out their missions, bombers must evade enemy defenses located near the targeted area. Similarly, ballistic missiles—ICBMs and SLBMs—must be able to penetrate any ABM system or other defense technology. Scientific developments in both areas could affect the performance of these forces in the future.

Bombers

Currently, low-flying American bombers are able to penetrate Soviet air defenses, which cannot at present readily distinguish aircraft from ground clutter on their radar. The forthcoming deployment of Soviet *look-down, shoot-down systems*—airborne radar and associated missiles that can detect and destroy low-altitude targets—could change this picture, jeopardizing the viability of the U.S. bomber force in the future.

The desire to maintain effective manned bombers—the only nuclear forces that can be dispatched, then recalled—is leading American technicians to examine ways of enhancing bomber penetration. One proposed solution calls for the replacement of the B-52 with the *B-1 bomber.* In flight over the Soviet Union, the B-1's smaller radar cross section, lower flight altitude, greater speed, and increased deceptive electronic countermeasures could reduce its vulnerability to

Soviet air defenses. Some scientists, however, have questioned the technical advantages of the B-1. They contend that test data suggest problems with the plane's acceleration, maneuverability, maintenance, and visibility to enemy defenses. Moreover, its penetration capabilities may be short-lived in the face of expected Soviet advances in air defense technology.

Given these doubts about the B-1, researchers are directing greater efforts toward a second technical solution: the refinement of a low-detection *stealth technology* that alters aircraft design and composition to make it virtually invisible to radar. Ultimately, such technology may be applied to a new generation of large aircraft; currently, stealth features are being incorporated in the U.S. cruise missile program.

Nuclear-armed *cruise missiles* are small, unmanned airplanes that can be launched from trucks, ships, submarines, or bombers. Their terrain-following guidance system allows them to fly low and use hills and valleys to cover their approach to target. In addition, on-board computers continually update the preprogrammed flight information, steering the cruise missile on course to achieve pinpoint targeting precision.

These features are leading some defense planners to advocate the deployment of thousands of *air-* and *sea-launched cruise missiles* (known as *ALCMs* and *SLCMs*) as well as hundreds of *ground-launched cruise missiles* (*GLCMs*) in Europe. This modernization program, embraced by the Reagan Administration, is prompting many observers to reexamine the merits of cruise missiles. "The Soviet Union may at some time in the future devise threat systems that place the current generation of ALCMs at risk, diminishing its effectiveness to an unacceptable level," notes a General Accounting Office report issued in February 1982. Such threats include the new look-down, shoot-down radar as well as modern surface-to-air missiles that can intercept low-flying ALCMs.

In addition to these concerns, doubts also have been raised regarding the implications of cruise missiles for nuclear stability. Although their limited range and slow speed make them suitable for retaliatory missions, cruise missiles may be upgraded in the future with greater ranges, speeds, and warhead characteristics that offer first-strike capability. Moreover, the flexible nature of cruise missiles—the fact that they can be launched from any platform, armed with nuclear or conventional warheads, and easily hidden because of their small size—creates dangerous uncertainty regarding enemy force capabilities and complicates efforts to monitor compliance with arms control agreements.

Although the United States currently leads in cruise missile technology, anticipated Soviet advances could create a situation akin to the early 1970s. At that time, notes former State Department official Leslie Gelb, ". . . the United States had the lead in missiles with multiple warheads, but the Soviets caught up and the new technology came back to haunt America."

Many defense officials nevertheless are wedded to the deployment of air-launched cruise missiles as an answer to the problem of bomber penetration. Regarding sea-launched cruise missiles, however, the notion of self-restraint—or negotiated restraint—is receiving considerable attention among arms control specialists. As John Newhouse, an assistant director of the Arms Control and Disarmament Agency in the Carter Administration, writes in *The New Yorker*:

> The new cruise missiles will give the arms competition another dimension and arms control possibly insoluble problems. . . . [C]ruise missiles are easy to hide and very difficult to monitor, particularly when they are deployed at sea—whether in ships or in submarines. . . . A class of unverifiable weapons—thousands of them—should be a sobering prospect.

Ballistic Missiles

Today, military planners have high confidence in the ability of ballistic missiles, including ICBMs and SLBMs, to reach enemy targets. The ABM Treaty of 1972 constrains the United States and the Soviet Union from deploying defensive systems that could undermine the effectiveness of a retaliatory attack. In both countries, however, research and development is being conducted at a rapid pace in several areas of *ballistic missile defense (BMD)* technology.

One system, under development at the time of the ABM Treaty negotiations, tracks an incoming warhead with radar to sort out any accompanying decoys, then fires a "defensive" nuclear warhead to destroy the attacking weapon. Another system, now under development, would carry many accurate *anti-missile missiles;* in essence, this design would "MIRV" the defensive system so that it could not be saturated by multiple warheads on incoming ICBMs. In the more distant future, *directed-energy weapons,* such as high energy lasers and particle beams, theoretically could be deployed in space to attack the other side's ICBMs as they were launched.

Corresponding to these developments in defense technology are efforts to *counter* threats to ballistic missile penetration. Possible technical solutions include upgrading decoys and other penetration aids, increasing the number of incoming warheads to tax the BMD system, and hardening ICBMs to make them less vulnerable to laser beams. Finally, nations could deploy *anti-satellite missiles (ASATs)* or space mines, capable of destroying space vehicles bearing defensive lasers.

Since 1967 the Soviet Union has been testing a low-altitude ASAT—a technology that the United States is expected to match and surpass by the middle of this decade. The ominous prospect of military competition in space is leading many policymakers to explore opportunities for arms control in this area. One obvious step is for American and Soviet leaders to abide by their commitment to the ABM Treaty and avoid any actions that would lead to its modification or abrogation. A second, more challenging avenue of arms control is presented by ASAT negotiations. In 1978, U.S.-Soviet negotiations aimed at limiting anti-satellite weapons were started, and some progress was achieved. Following the Soviet invasion of Afghanistan in late 1979, however, the talks were suspended indefinitely, and the Reagan Administration has refused to resume negotiations on this subject since it took office. In the absence of agreement, both the United States and the Soviet Union are likely to expand their ASAT programs, thus triggering new concerns about the controllability of nuclear forces.

■ Technology and Controllability

The controllability of nuclear forces is a vital and yet often overlooked feature of American and Soviet nuclear arsenals. The network of links comprising the command and control system—known to American military planners as C^3I for *command, control, communication and intelligence*—serves several critical functions. It provides the warning system for alerting nuclear forces and evacuating national leaders, it provides the coordinating mechanism for "battle management" and the execution of orders during attack, and it provides warring nations with the central ability to "turn the war off" and end hostilities. The survivability of the U.S. command system thus is considered essential to deterrence: without it, American strategic forces cannot be coordinated to retaliate in the event of a nuclear attack.

Unfortunately, the command network, writes John Steinbruner of the Brookings Institution, "is at once the most vulnerable and valuable strategic target." Its vulnerability can be traced to many factors. For example, the early warning systems that detect an attack—such as radar sites and satellite sensor equipment—are relatively soft targets and hence vulnerable to nuclear blast. The command centers that assess and verify warning data—such as the headquarters for the North American Air Defense (NORAD) and the Strategic Air Command (SAC)—are located in fixed sites and unlikely to withstand a direct nuclear attack. The communications links—such as land cables, sea cables, and satellite and radio systems—that connect the president, the command posts, and the nuclear forces are susceptible to electronic jamming and other forms of interference. Most importantly, the structure for implementing retaliatory decisions—the National Command Authority (NCA) consisting of the president, the secretary of Defense, and their delegates or successors—is highly vulnerable in the event of attack, raising serious doubts about the continuity of decision-making authority during a nuclear war.

Two recent trends in weapons technology are exacerbating the vulnerabilities of C³I systems both in the United States and the Soviet Union. First, the growing reliance on short-time-of-flight weapons that can reach enemy command centers within minutes places both governments at an increased risk of "decapitation." From the Soviet perspective, this danger is posed by the introduction of American Pershing II missiles in Europe and the possible future deployment of Trident II ballistic missiles on submarines near the Soviet Union. Most ominous, from the U.S. viewpoint, are Soviet missiles on submarines near the American coastline and the threatened deployment of so-called *depressed-trajectory* sea-launched missiles that fly at low angles to shorten their flight times. According to many defense specialists, these developments could lead the United States and the Soviet Union to adopt policies to mitigate the effects of a decapitation attack on national leaders. Either or both nations could plan, for example, to launch on warning and fire their weapons upon receiving signals that enemy missiles are en route. Or they could move toward *pre-delegation* of firing authority, allowing military personnel to initiate the use of nuclear weapons without consulting the nation's civilian leadership. Although such measures might reduce ambiguity in the command of nuclear forces, the increased reliance on computers and military officers could heighten the risk of nuclear war.

A second unsettling trend is posed by the growing militarization of space. Advances in anti-satellite warfare and other forms of space weaponry cast doubt on the future viability of satellite systems that aid the command and control of nuclear forces. This threat is particularly troublesome from the standpoint of the United States, which is highly dependent on satellites to relay its military messages around the world.

Trends in space technology, coupled with the increasing potency and speed of weapons targeted at command centers, are leading many defense officials to advocate improvements in C³I facilities and the development of more "resilient" military satellites. The Reagan Administration has identified these measures as the number one priority in its strategic modernization program. Such steps, it is claimed, will not only improve national security but also enhance global stability by reducing the risk of accidental nuclear war.

To the same end, many legislators and arms control specialists believe that U.S.-Soviet negotiations should be pursued with greater vigor to increase confidence in the command and control of both sides' nuclear forces. Current suggestions include restricting the deployment of short-time-of-flight weapons targeted at national command centers and banning operational tests of anti-satellite weapons.

In many respects, the continuing debate over space weaponry reflects a fundamental question about military technology—whether new weapons, in the long run, increase or decrease the risk of nuclear war. Currently, the perceived advantages of exploiting space technology—including anti-satellite weapons and space-based ABM systems—are leading some government officials to seek further acceleration of American programs in these areas. Many others, aware of U.S. reliance on military and non-military satellites, fear that the United States has more to lose in an anti-satellite battle than the Soviet Union. Moreover, they recognize the expense and danger of expanding the superpowers' arms race to this new "high ground."

In resolving the space weapons debate, the essential issue, as in other areas of nuclear arms policy, is whether American interests are better served in an environment shaped by negotiated agreements or by unchecked technological competition. Given the risks created by new weapons systems, it may be that arms control is the safer route, that there is, in the words of columnist Flora Lewis, "no answer but negotiation, no magic technological formula man can devise to remove the danger of holocaust already devised, no likely 'breakthrough' that could settle the balance for good."

■ Selected Sources

Desmond Ball, "Counterforce Targeting: How New? How Viable?", *Arms Control Today* (The Arms Control Association, February 1981).

Philip M. Boffey, "Trident's Technology May Make It a Potent Rival to Land-Based Missiles," *The New York Times,* July 13, 1982.

Paul Bracken, *The Command and Control of Nuclear Forces* (Yale University Press, 1983).

Harvey Brooks, "The Military Innovation System and the Qualitative Arms Race," *Daedalus: Arms, Defense Policy, and Arms Control* (Journal of the American Academy of Arts and Sciences, Summer 1975).

McGeorge Bundy, "MX Paper: Appealing, But Mostly Appalling," *The New York Times,* April 17, 1983.

Congressional Budget Office, *Modernizing U.S. Strategic Offensive Forces: The Administration's Program and Alternatives* (U.S. Government Printing Office, May 1983).

Richard L. Garwin, "Will Strategic Submarines Be Vulnerable?" *International Security,* Fall 1983.

Albert Gore, Jr., "The Fork in the Road," *The New Republic,* May 5, 1982.

Richard Halloran, "Buildup in Space: A New Military Focus," *The New York Times,* October 17, 1982 (see also the other articles in this series, October 18 and 19, 1982).

The Harvard Study Group, *Living with Nuclear Weapons* (Harvard University Press, 1983).

Fred Kaplan, "Cruise Missile: Wonder Weapon or Dud?", *High Technology,* February 1983.

Thomas Karas, *The New High Ground: Strategies and Weapons of Space-Age War* (Simon and Schuster, 1983).

William H. Kincade, "Over the Technological Horizon," *Daedalus: U.S. Policy in the 1980's* (Journal of the American Academy of Arts and Sciences, Winter 1981).

Henry Kissinger, "A New Approach to Arms Control, *Time,* March 21, 1983.

Charles Mohr, "Cruise Missile Passes Tests but Its Critics Score Too," *The New York Times,* July 17, 1983.

William J. Perry, "Advanced Technology and Arms Control," *ORBIS,* Summer 1982.

———, "Technological Prospects," in *Rethinking the U.S. Strategic Posture,* edited by Barry M. Blechman (Aspen Institute, 1982).

Jeffrey Porro, "BMD Technology: A Layman's Guide," *Arms Control Today* (The Arms Control Association, April 1981).

Report of the President's Commission on Strategic Forces, April 1983.

R. Jeffrey Smith, "An Upheaval in U.S. Strategic Thought," *Science,* April 2, 1982 (see also the other articles in this series, April 9, 16, 23, 30, May 7 and 21, 1982).

John Steinbruner, "Arms and the Art of Compromise," *The Brookings Review,* Summer 1983.

Joel Wit, "'Sanctuaries' and Security: Suggestions for ASW Arms Control," *Arms Control Today* (The Arms Control Association, October 1980).

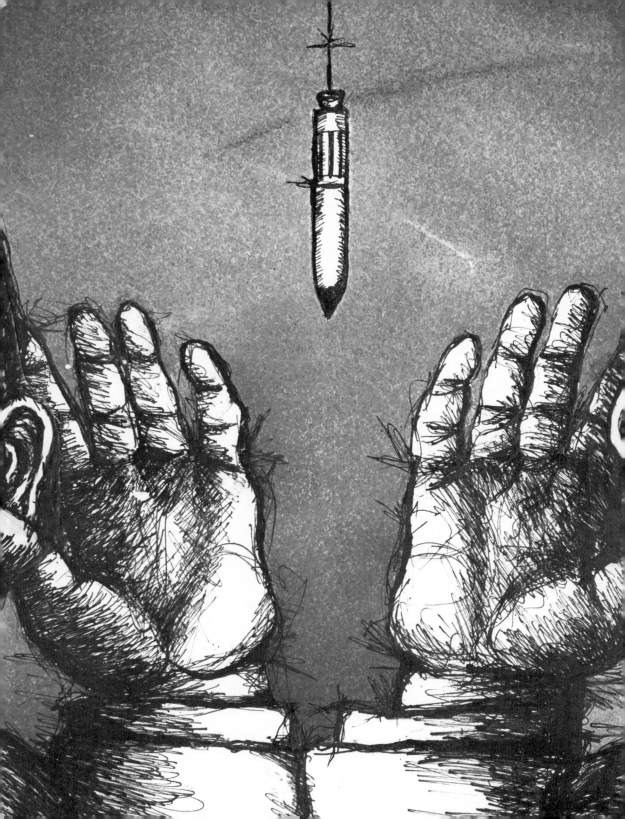

IV. HOW SHOULD WE DEAL WITH THE SOVIET UNION?

The final lesson of the Cuban missile crisis is the importance of placing ourselves in the other country's shoes.

Robert F. Kennedy
1967

Can the United States Verify Soviet Treaty Compliance?

Today, most Americans view arms control as a path to greater security, yet often are uncomfortable at the thought of negotiating with the Soviet Union. To a large extent, public ambivalence about arms control can be traced to doubts about the reliability of Soviet leaders to keep their word. "The American people don't want to be snookered," notes Albert Carnesale, a member of the SALT I negotiating team and now a professor at Harvard University.

Despite this concern about "trusting the Russians," most citizens are unfamiliar with the process of detecting and challenging violations of arms control agreements. Instead, information on the ability of the United States to verify Soviet treaty compliance is confined to intelligence experts and not understood by the public at large. As a result, public debate over verification is often superficial and highly polarized. Author John Prados explains this problem in his book *The Soviet Estimate:*

> Most information, particularly if it is of an alarming nature, generally reaches the public in a more or less watered-down fashion within six months to a year of its appearance at the intelligence-community level. Such information normally appears in a scattered and desultory way and because, by and large, the public is not really equipped to evaluate it, it usually helps to create or to further reinforce a hostile image of the adversary.

The dangers of the nuclear age, however, demand that we contract with our adversary on matters of national survival. In this context, the public's understanding of the verification debate is crucial to its confidence in the arms control process.

■ The Process of Verification

The challenge of assessing Soviet treaty compliance frequently is perceived as a technical problem to be "solved" objectively by technical experts. Yet the process of *verification* has several complex facets. It includes collecting information or intelligence about Soviet activities, evaluating the data in relation to the terms of the treaty, and responding to adverse Soviet behavior through enforcement and grievance procedures. This range of activity by the U.S. government—involving both factfinding and policymaking—highlights the dual nature of the verification process. Ultimately, politics, as well as science, plays a role in the debate over Soviet compliance and reflects fundamental value judgments about U.S. national security.

Factfinding: Monitoring Soviet Weapons Programs

The United States continuously tracks Soviet military activities, regardless of whether an arms control agreement is in place. The existence of a treaty, however, imposes specific limits on Soviet weapons programs, which then must be monitored by U.S. intelligence. Moreover, the text of a treaty may enumerate specific ground rules to aid the factfinding process, thus improving American surveillance capabilities.

The United States relies on two basic methods for monitoring Soviet nuclear weapons programs: national technical means and cooperative methods of verification.

National Technical Means

In the words of Robert Kaiser, former Moscow bureau chief for *The Washington Post, national technical means (NTM)* is "a euphemism for finding out what the Russians are doing without any help from the Russians." The term refers to technical methods of data collection—including satellite cameras, radio interceptors, and ground radar—that do not require active cooperation by the nation under surveillance. These internationally-recognized means of intelligence first gained acceptance in the 1972 ABM Treaty between the United States and the Soviet Union. At the same time, the two nations agreed in principle to refrain from interfering with national technical means by deliberately concealing activities essential to verification.

The U.S. monitoring effort is geared toward detecting and describing Soviet nuclear weapons in terms of their quantity and quality. *Satellite cameras* are the primary source of quantitative information about Soviet weapons programs. This technology can locate, count, and measure operational missile launchers as well as those under construction. Two types of satellites are used for this mission. *Search-and-find satellites* provide complete photographic coverage of the Soviet Union in a single day, surveying wide areas at frequent intervals. If suspicious activity is detected at a known or discovered weapons site, *close-look satellites* can zoom in to provide a clearer, more detailed picture. Herbert Scoville, Jr., former CIA Deputy Director for Science and Technology, describes this capability:

U.S. Monitoring Capabilities: How They Come Together

"To illustrate the difficulties of clandestine deployment (and the capabilities of the U.S. intelligence collection system) one need only trace the lifetime of a Soviet ICBM from design through deployment. It is known that the Soviets have four design bureaus for the deployment of their ICBMs. United States intelligence monitors the nature of the projects and the technologies pursued at these bureaus. It is generally known which bureau is working on each new or significantly modified ICBM under development, and analysts have a reasonably good idea of when the Soviets will begin flight-testing these missiles.

"The United States regularly monitors key areas at the Soviet ICBM test ranges. Missile test firings are monitored with a wide variety of sensors: cameras taking pictures of launch and impact areas; infrared detectors measuring heat from the engine; radars tracking ICBMs in flight; and radios receiving Soviet telemetry signals. In the course of 20 to 30 tests of a new ICBM, the United States collects thousands of reels of magnetic tape and analysts spend tens of thousands of hours processing, analyzing, and correlating this vast array of data to determine the new missile's characteristics.

"Missile production takes place at several main assembly

. . . it is quite feasible to differentiate between a launch complex for the large Soviet SS-18 missile and one for its somewhat smaller SS-19. The lateral dimensions can be measured quite accurately, probably within a foot, so that any change in its maximum size can be determined.

To deal with unfavorable surveillance conditions, such as darkness, camouflage, or underground activity, satellites are equipped with modern devices to supplement standard means of photography. For example, a special camera, known as a *multi-spectral scanner,* can produce an image in electronic, digital form that then can be enhanced by computer techniques to create a highly-detailed color photo. If this technology were used to distinguish silo covers camouflaged by green paint from the surrounding foliage, for example, the paint would appear blue and the leaves, bright red. Picture-like images also can be formed by *thermal infrared scanners* that can measure temperature differences between a suspicious object and the surrounding terrain. With this technology, underground silos or construction stand out in an infrared picture.

Qualitative information about Soviet weapons programs is collected primarily by U.S. *radio interceptors.* Listening posts continually monitor radio signals that are transmitted by Soviet missiles, during flight tests, to ground receivers. These signals, known as *telemetry,* are designed to provide the Soviets with a detailed data base for assessing the reliability of their missile system. Intercepted by the United States, the telemetry provides valuable intelligence about weapon performance and design, including the throw-weight and range of the missile, the type of fuel propelling its flight, and the number, kind, and accuracy of the re-entry vehicles it releases.

United States eavesdropping on Soviet communications could be impeded by deceptive measures that encode, or encrypt, Soviet radio signals. During SALT II, however, both nations recognized the value of telemetry for monitoring treaty compliance. Accordingly, the use of telemetry encryption to impede verification efforts was forbidden by the signed, but unratified, agreement.

Soviet flight tests also are monitored by *ground radar* facilities that beam radio waves at the missile in flight to determine its path and velocity as well as its design. The United States operates two basic types of ground sites. *Line-of-sight radar* can identify the distinctive pattern of reflected microwaves associated with each major type of Soviet missile. Limited in scope by the curve of the earth, these radar stations must be located as close as possible to Soviet test ranges. *Over-the-horizon radar* can bounce signals over a greater distance and recognize the distinctive "signature" of each missile as it disturbs the upper atmosphere.

In addition to ground stations, *surveillance ships and planes* carry radar, as well as infrared and optical sensors, for a variety of intelligence missions. With successive flyovers, U.S. aircraft can detect changes in strategic programs along Soviet coasts and borders. As moving "spy" platforms, U.S. naval vessels can position themselves close to the point of impact during Soviet missile tests and provide detailed information on Soviet reentry vehicles.

Information about strategic nuclear forces in the Soviet Union thus can be drawn from a variety of national technical means. "This intelligence system," writes Joseph Kruzel, a member of the SALT I delegation, "is highly sophisticated, overlapping, and well-coordinated." He explains:

> What is learned from one source—photography, for example—can often be checked against information from other sources such as radar or telemetry monitoring. The use of multiple sources complicates any effort to disguise or conceal a violation.

Most intelligence specialists acknowledge the considerable success of U.S. detection equipment in tracking Soviet weapons systems. Nevertheless, it generally is recognized that technical surveillance methods are neither "all-seeing" nor equally suited to all missions. As Robert Kaiser observes, "On a purely technical level, national means of detection remain one of the miracles of our age. . . . We have an extraordinary ringside seat on the whole Soviet program." Nevertheless, notes Kaiser:

> . . . limitations on the production of weapons and on the qualitative aspects of weapons . . . by their nature, cannot be spied upon from satellites in the sky or eavesdropped upon by great earphones in the sky, but must be examined in other ways, involving Soviet cooperation . . . .

A report prepared by a panel of strategic experts for the Carnegie Endowment for International Peace identifies several stages in the development of a weapons system that are difficult to monitor by independent means. There is, for example, less certainty in tracking the pre-flight test stage of development, the rate and scale of production and deployment, or the extent to which missiles actually are equipped with multiple warheads. Technical methods of monitoring these activities are aided by traditional sources of intelligence, such as spies and defectors. Nevertheless, U.S.-Soviet verification could be aided significantly by greater reliance on cooperative measures.

plants and at hundreds of sub-assembly plants, employing hundreds of thousands of workers. U.S. collectors monitor the Soviet ICBM deployment areas on a regular basis, observing construction activity, movement of people and materials, and training exercises. The intelligence community has a good understanding of the organizational and support structure for deployed ICBM units.

"Silo launchers for ICBMs are readily identifiable during construction and take a year or more to build. The missiles themselves require extensive support facilities, including missile-handling equipment, checkout and maintenance facilities, and survivable communications. The nuclear warheads require special handling, storage, and security facilities. U.S. intelligence collectors regularly examine the existing ICBM fields, but they also conduct extensive surveys of the Soviet Union at periodic intervals for evidence of additional ICBM activity.

"It is inconceivable that the Soviets could perform any significant part of this process of designing, testing, and deploying an ICBM without being detected by the United States. ICBMs and the nuclear warheads they carry are not small toys that can be easily concealed. They are large, fragile, and dangerous systems requiring a major effort to build, and they pose an almost impossible task of significant concealment."

—from "Verification and SALT II" by Joseph Kruzel, published in *Verification and SALT,* edited by William C. Potter. Used by permission of Westview Press, ©1980 by William C. Potter.

Verifying a Nuclear Arms Freeze

There is considerable debate over the issue of whether a nuclear arms freeze between the United States and the Soviet Union could be verified with confidence. To some observers, the scope of the freeze would be a liability, placing unrealistic demands on U.S. monitoring capabilities in difficult areas of production and deployment, as well as testing. To others, its comprehensive nature would be an asset, rendering any activity in a proscribed area immediately suspect. Both sides concur that a freeze agreement necessarily would involve independent and cooperative methods of verification.

Testifying before Congress in 1983 on behalf of a freeze, former CIA Director William Colby said:

A freeze might indeed require some additional intelligence coverage in order to be fully verifiable. Our intelligence today provides general estimates of such matters as the production of nuclear weapons, but a freeze might call for more precise assurances that such production fully stops.

The problems of obtaining such assurances, however, can be negotiated and additional monitoring arrangements made to provide them. Electronic sensors emplaced in appro-

Cooperative Methods of Verification

The United States and the Soviet Union currently rely on "passive" means of cooperation to aid the surveillance missions of both countries. The prohibitions on deliberate concealment and telemetry encryption are examples of mutual efforts to avoid active deception. In a similar vein, the unratified SALT II agreement sets forth affirmative steps to aid the factfinding process. For example, one provision calls for the routine exchange of data on forces that would enable each nation to double-check its independent information against an *agreed data base.* Another requires the United States and Soviet Union to design certain aircraft with *functionally-related observable differences,* such as externally mounted missiles, to facilitate identification by satellite. In addition, *counting rules* are provided to simplify verification of the treaty's ceilings on multiple warheads. Under these guidelines, any missile that is ever tested with MIRVs or any launcher that launches a MIRVed missile is counted toward the MIRV ceiling, even if it is deployed with only one warhead. Although these steps, as well as others established by SALT II, involve some degree of cooperation, they primarily are designed to bolster national technical means of surveillance.

By contrast, the term *cooperative methods of verification* specifically refers to measures that require active participation by the nation under surveillance and territorial access for the observing country. Two types of procedures commonly are discussed in this context: seismic stations and on-site inspections.

Seismic stations, known as "black boxes," are automatic devices that can measure underground events and can distinguish between phenomena such as earthquakes and nuclear weapons test explosions. Although remote stations, located outside the country under surveillance, can gather substantial seismic data, black boxes placed inside the territory can provide more accurate information on low-yield nuclear tests conducted under unusual conditions. This information then can be authenticated by devices within the tamper-proof seismic station and transmitted back to orbiting satellites.

On-site inspection refers to the process of sending inspectors into another country to monitor military activities. Such investigations can be limited to *challenge inspections,* in which outside personnel are sent in to clarify ambiguous information detected by national technical means. Or they can be more intrusive in nature, involving unscheduled visits and even a constant presence at specific military sites.

These cooperative methods of verification, however useful, currently are unavailable to the United States and the Soviet Union. Such arrangements are difficult to negotiate and have met with resistance by Soviet leaders who, like some American military officials, regard on-site inspection as an infringement of national sovereignty. The Soviet Union has preferred instead to supplement its intelligence apparatus with the public documents that are readily available on American strategic programs, such as Defense Department reports, Congressional hearing records, and trade journals. Comparable sources of military data on Soviet programs have been unavailable to the United States because of the Soviet government's rigid control of the flow of information. Commenting on this problem, William Colby, Director of the Central Intelligence Agency from 1973 to 1976, observes:

> The Soviets are never going to have the kind of open society that we have, nor will there ever be a Moscow edition of *Aviation Week,* but I believe that these are issues subject to negotiation, and that the Soviets have moved in the necessary direction.

The basis for optimism about cooperative verification stems from the recent history of negotiations concerning nuclear explosions. In the introduction to the unratified 1976 Treaty on Peaceful Nuclear Explosions (PNE), the United States and the Soviet Union agreed to detailed on-site inspection procedures. These procedures were incorporated, in principle, into subsequent negotiations among the United States, the Soviet Union, and Great Britain for a Comprehensive Test Ban Treaty (CTB) on all underground tests. (Aboveground testing already was prohibited by the 1963 Limited Test Ban Treaty.) Unfortunately, the CTB negotiations subsequently were suspended by President Reagan in 1981. The Administration cited three reasons for reaching its decision: its doubts about verification, its concern about the Soviet compliance record to date, and its interest in further weapons testing.

Despite this development, the CTB negotiations offer evidence of progress in Soviet attitudes toward cooperative verification. During these talks, the Soviet Union accepted the American proposal to install ten black boxes in Soviet territory. Moreover, they began to negotiate on detailed procedures for actual conduct of on-site inspections. According to former U.S. negotiator Alan Niedle, success in gaining Soviet agreement to these points was based on the convincing technical case for on-site measures that, in turn, enabled the United States to negotiate from a strong political position. Writes Niedle:

> The CTB experience is quite encouraging. The Soviets' acceptance of ten tamper-proof seismic stations in their territory would really have been like strapping a giant lie detector around the Soviet Union. It would have

priate places, inspection visits to suspected areas, arrangements for third party or neutral determination of questions raised, all offer possible vehicles to provide the necessary assurances. It is too easy to say that the Soviets would not agree to such arrangements, as they have dropped their opposition to these kinds of procedures when shown the necessity for them.

been a first in history, and I think it's really worth working for in the future.

Whatever the prospects for greater cooperation, emerging changes in strategic weapon design will pose new challenges to verification efforts. For example, the increasing availability of "dual-capable" systems that can be armed with either conventional or nuclear warheads, and the growing mobility of nuclear weapons—trends embodied in the development of the cruise missile—will complicate surveillance and heighten the need for cooperative measures. It is likely, nevertheless, that national technical means will remain the cornerstone of U.S. factfinding efforts. To a large extent, this reliance on NTM reflects the confidence of U.S. intelligence officials in our independent detection capabilities. In the words of Harold Brown, Secretary of Defense in the Carter Administration:

> It is inconceivable to me that the Soviets could develop, produce, test, and deploy a new ICBM in a way that would evade this monitoring network. We have missed some data on some firings—and will in the future. But we have not erred significantly in our assessment of any Soviet ICBM.

The recent report by strategic specialists prepared for the Carnegie Endowment for International Peace supports this view:

> While it is true by definition that our NTM have never found anything the Soviets have successfully hidden, it is also true that there are remarkably few instances of concealments of development and deployment that worked for a considerable time before discovery—which would be the pattern expected with widespread, quite successful concealment efforts. . . . [I]n terms of reporting actual events, the intelligence record is quite good. No new Soviet strategic systems . . . have ever been deployed, without our having known about them in advance.

Policymaking: Assessing and Enforcing Soviet Compliance

The United States has numerous procedures in place to evaluate information on weapons developments in the Soviet Union. The Central Intelligence Agency, the Defense Intelligence Agency, the Department of State, and the National Security Agency all participate in the process of analyzing observed Soviet behavior. The existence of an arms control treaty focuses the interagency efforts on a specific mission: to determine whether the monitored activity is consistent with the terms of the agreement.

The current controversy over Soviet treaty compliance

highlights the subjective nature of this seemingly objective process. The meaning of Soviet actions can be difficult to assess for several reasons. First, technical information on Soviet weapons developments may be incomplete or inconsistent. Given the variety of data collectors, such as radar and satellites, evidence of non-compliance may be ambiguous, particularly in the early stages of evaluation.

Second, the detected activity, however certain its occurrence, may be subject to conflicting interpretations. For example, some U.S. analysts may view a change in a Soviet missile system as a permissible "modification" under the terms of the treaty; others may regard it as a prohibited form of modernization.

Third, the relevant provisions of a negotiated agreement may be vague or ambiguous. The loosely-worded ban on telemetry encryption in the SALT II Treaty, for example, leaves room for debate: If the Soviets encode their radio signals, are they necessarily taking steps to "impede verification efforts?" Indeed, treaty language sometimes is kept deliberately imprecise to secure general agreement by both parties, to preserve flexibility, and to encompass a wide range of activities too numerous to mention.

As these issues demonstrate, the process of assessing Soviet compliance with arms control agreements is neither clear-cut nor automatic, but depends on the judgment of policy-level decisionmakers. The findings and recommendations of the intelligence community are reported to the president by the director of the Central Intelligence Agency. The Administration then decides whether and how to raise the issue of suspicious activity with the Soviet Union. The decision to use formal grievance procedures—often stipulated in the treaty text—or informal, back-door channels of communication may depend on any number of factors: the strength of the available evidence, the seriousness of the suspected violation, the state of U.S.-Soviet relations, and the extent to which raising an issue compromises U.S. intelligence capabilities.

Faced with evidence of a possible treaty violation, the United States may request official clarification of Soviet actions in the *Standing Consultative Commission (SCC)*. Created in 1972 under SALT I, the SCC is a joint U.S.-Soviet forum that deals with arms control compliance questions. The commission has jurisdiction over the ABM Treaty, the SALT I Interim Agreement, and the unratified SALT II Treaty. Each government is represented by a commissioner, a deputy commissioner, and other advisors who participate in confidential meetings at least twice a year.

The SCC process may serve to resolve the disputed matter

to the satisfaction of both delegations. In some instances, however, an aggrieved nation may take further steps to redress its grievances against an alleged violator, including formal diplomatic protests, countermeasures through weapons programs, emergency military action, or withdrawal from the treaty.

In selecting a policy response to Soviet violations, the United States government must determine which course of action is most appropriate and timely. "Appropriate," notes Joseph Kruzel, "means that the response should match the violation in terms of strategic significance." "[T]imely," he explains, "means that the U.S. response should come in time to deny or offset the advantage the Soviet Union would expect to gain from the act of violation." Such criteria inevitably reflect the views of the policymaker regarding what constitutes adequate verification.

■ The Debate Over Adequate Verification

Concern about U.S. verification capabilities generally stems from a desire for certainty—certainty in detecting Soviet misconduct, certainty in holding such conduct accountable, and certainty in enforcing Soviet compliance. Even the most sophisticated procedures for verification are not 100 percent certain—a fact that drives the entire verification debate. When we ask if an arms control treaty is verifiable, we really are asking whether our less-than-perfect means for verification are *adequate*.

The concept of adequate verification is easily amenable to manipulation by supporters and opponents of a particular arms control measure. Despite its politicization, the concept has a bipartisan history. It was used by President Nixon in his instructions to the first SALT delegation and repeatedly endorsed by subsequent administrations. During the Senate hearings on SALT II, then-Secretary of Defense Harold Brown offered his oft-quoted interpretation of this approach:

> No arms limitation agreement can ever be absolutely verifiable. The relevant test is not an abstract ideal, but the practical standard of whether we can determine compliance adequately to safeguard our security—that is, whether we can identify attempted evasion if it occurs on a large enough scale to pose a significant risk, and whether we can do so in time to mount a sufficient response. Meeting this test is what I mean by the term "adequate verification."

The actual "scale" of cheating thus colors any judgment of U.S. verification capabilities. Policymakers reasonably may differ over the military implications of a given Soviet action.

Nevertheless, most observers concur that the present U.S.-Soviet strategic balance will not be affected by minor violations. Former CIA Director William Colby explains:

> In a world with 50,000 nuclear weapons, it is hard to imagine that the secret development of a few more would change the balance of power, even though it might be a breach of contract. . . . Any program which offered the prospect of a strategic advantage to the Soviets by definition would have to be of a size and consequent visibility that we could identify it before it became a direct threat . . . .

As Colby suggests, small-scale evasions, although difficult to detect, lack military significance; large-scale evasions, on the other hand, invite detection as well as unfavorable political repercussions. Taken together, these factors pose a formidable disincentive for cheating. An international panel of experts—known as the "Palme Commission"—supports this view in their 1982 report entitled *Common Security: A Blueprint for Survival*:

> Violation of an agreement based on adequate verification of compliance would entail a risk of detection, and therefore a danger of jeopardizing the agreement in question and political relations among the parties to the treaty. If agreements reflect mutual interests, a violation of them would amount to a violation of self-interest.

■ The Soviet Record of Treaty Compliance

"I do not believe that the Soviets would enter into any agreement which required them to cheat in order to attain their military objectives, or on which they planned to cheat," said Sidney Graybeal, former U.S. representative to the Standing Consultative Commission, at a Senate hearing in 1979. There is, however, considerable controversy surrounding the Soviet record of treaty compliance to date. At issue are several pacts dealing with nuclear arms control—the SALT I accords, the unratified SALT II Treaty, and two test ban treaties—as well as international agreements on biological and chemical warfare.

SALT I Accords

In February 1978, the Department of State released a public report on SALT I compliance. Prepared in response to a Senate committee request and with the tacit approval of the Soviet Union, the report summarized issues addressed during the classified proceedings of the Standing Consultative Commission.

The document discusses eight questions raised by the United States regarding Soviet compliance with SALT I and five questions raised by the Soviet Union regarding U.S. compliance. Three areas of American concern reflect the type of problem addressed and resolved by the SCC:

Launch control facilities: In 1973, the U.S. observed the possible construction of new silos for land-based missiles in violation of SALT I. A Soviet response that the facilities were built to house personnel for launch control programs subsequently was confirmed by U.S. intelligence. Discussion of the matter was closed by the U.S. in 1977.

Air defense system radar: In 1973 and 1974, the U.S. observed a Soviet radar tracking a missile in test flight, indicating a possible effort to use the radar for missile defenses, in violation of the ABM treaty. Although maintaining that the radar had a different, permissible mission, the Soviets curtailed the activity shortly after the issue was discussed by the SCC.

Modern, large ballistic missiles: In early 1975, the U.S. questioned the Soviets' deployment of their large SS-19 missile, a step considered inconsistent with SALT I's ban on converting "light" ICBM launchers to "heavy" ICBM launchers. The U.S. issued its own interpretation of "heavy" during SALT I, but the treaty contained no agreed-upon definition. As a result, deployment was permitted, and the treaty language subsequently was clarified in SALT II.

The record in SALT I reflects a mixed pattern of Soviet behavior, including a willingness to exploit ambiguities and a disregard for unilateral interpretations issued by the United States. In the past, complaints regarding Soviet behavior generally have resulted in the cessation of the objectionable activity or a satisfactory explanation of it. The recent construction of a large Soviet radar installation in Siberia, however, raises new questions about Soviet compliance and suggests a possible violation of provisions of the ABM Treaty. The Reagan Administration reportedly has raised this issue in the SCC.

SALT II Treaty

The unratified status of the SALT II Treaty clouds the compliance question. Despite public allegations of Soviet misconduct, the Reagan Administration was reluctant until recently to raise any formal grievances before the Standing Consultative Commission—an act that would constitute acceptance of the unratified treaty. Controversy surrounding SALT II stems largely from early reports of Soviet missile tests that suggest, to some officials, possible violations of the treaty's limit on the testing and deployment of one new type of ICBM as well as the ban on telemetry encryption during missile tests. Other policymakers, however, take a different view of the available evidence. Rethinking its earlier posture, the Administration has submitted these issues to the SCC for discussion and resolution.

Test Ban Treaties

The Threshold Test Ban Treaty (TTB) bars the United States and Soviet Union from testing warheads with yields greater than 150 kilotons. Although the treaty was signed in 1974, its submission to the U.S. Senate was delayed pending the conclusion of a companion treaty in 1976 on peaceful nuclear explosions (PNE).

In 1982, President Reagan withdrew the TTB and PNE treaties from Senate consideration, citing his concern about alleged Soviet violations. According to Administration reports, Soviet tests may have exceeded the 150-kiloton threshold on 14 occasions since the treaties were signed.

These claims have been the subject of much debate in the scientific community. In October 1982, two seismologists, Drs. Lynn Sykes and Jack Evernden, co-authored an article in *Scientific American* examining the available evidence on Soviet testing. In their judgment, the debate over the size of Soviet tests revolves solely around the choice of scientific methods for obtaining yield estimates. Their research led them to this conclusion:

> Using mainly surface waves, we estimated yields of the larger Soviet explosions from 1976, the date that the Threshold Treaty went into effect, through October 1981. None of the computed yields were above the 150 kt threshold. While several of the Soviet tests were close to the 150 kt threshold, we find no evidence that the U.S.S.R. has violated the terms of the Threshold Treaty.

Other scientists take a contrary view, finding substantial evidence of high-yield testing by the Soviet Union. This discrepancy is not surprising to one Pentagon seismologist quoted in *Science* magazine:

> If you start with a philosophical bias that the Soviets are not cheating, the geological data are there to say that. If you start with a philosophical bias that they are cheating, the data are there to say that.

Ironically, the Administration's decision to withhold support for the PNE and TTB Treaties prevents the United States from utilizing the very provisions of those treaties that would enhance verification, especially in areas that evidence a relaxation of the Soviets' earlier positions. For example, the Soviets had agreed in principle to exchange geophysical data in connection with the Threshold Test Ban Treaty and were prepared to accept special on-site activities by foreign observers in the Peaceful Nuclear Explosions Treaty.

Agreements on Biological and Chemical Warfare

Serious charges of Soviet misconduct also arise in an area outside nuclear arms control—biological and chemical warfare. These activities are proscribed by two multilateral agreements to which the United States and the Soviet Union are parties: the Geneva Protocol of 1925 and the Biological Weapons Convention of 1972. Neither document, however, contains any detailed verification provisions.

Citing evidence of chemical warfare in Afghanistan and Southeast Asia, the United States in 1980 urged the General Assembly of the United Nations to initiate a formal inquiry into Soviet action. A final report, issued by a panel of experts in December of 1982, was less than definitive:

> While the group could not state that these allegations had been proven, nevertheless it could not disregard the circumstantial evidence suggestive of the possible use of some sort of toxic chemical substances in some instances.

The Soviets' lack of cooperation in clearing up these matters has reinforced—and in some ways legitimated—public doubts about Soviet intentions, despite their apparent compliance with other treaties. "These instances," according to the report prepared for the Carnegie Endowment for International Peace, are a "political time bomb under all future arms control agreements."

The controversy surrounding treaty compliance highlights the inherent uncertainties in verifying arms control agreements, the need for steady progress in negotiations, and the importance of cooperation among nuclear nations. As author John Prados observes in *The Soviet Estimate*, "The beginning of wisdom . . . lies in the realization that one must go beyond intelligence to cope with the problems of the arms race."

■ Selected Sources

Les Aspin, "The Verification of the SALT II Agreement," *Scientific American,* February 1979.

Carnegie Panel on U.S. Security and the Future of Arms Control, *Challenges for U.S. National Security* (Carnegie Endowment for International Peace, 1983).

Center for Defense Information, *Soviet Compliance with SALT I* (Center for Defense Information, 1982).

Department of State, "SALT One: Compliance; SALT Two: Verification," *Selected Documents* (Department of State, 1978).

Charles C. Floweree, "Chemical Weapons: A Case Study in Verification," *Arms Control Today* (The Arms Control Association, April 1983).

Michael R. Gordon, "Can Reagan Blow the Whistle on the Russians While Saying No on SALT II?" *National Journal,* May 7, 1983.

William H. Kincade, "Challenges to Verification: Old and New," *Arms Control: The Journal of Arms Control and Disarmament,* December 1982.

Mark M. Lowenthal, *SALT Verification* (Congressional Research Service, The Library of Congress, July 10, 1978).

Judith Miller, "Debate Over Nuclear Ban: Can U.S. Spot Cheats?", *The New York Times,* March 8, 1983.

William C. Potter, ed., *Verification and SALT: The Challenge of Strategic Deception* (Westview Press, 1980).

John Prados, *The Soviet Estimate: U.S. Intelligence Analysis and Russian Military Strength* (The Dial Press, 1982).

"Soviet Compliance with Arms Control Agreements," *Arms Control Today* (The Arms Control Association, March 1984).

Lynn R. Sykes and Jack F. Evernden, "The Verification of a Comprehensive Nuclear Test Ban," *Scientific American,* October 1982.

"Verifying a Model Freeze," *F.A.S. Public Interest Report* (Federation of American Scientists, September 1982).

Do the United States and the Soviet Union Have Mutual Interests?

Preventing nuclear war is not something the United States can do alone. The Soviet Union is our principal adversary in the world at present, and its actions also will determine whether or not a nuclear war occurs. The attitudes of Soviet leaders thus are a major factor for U.S. policymakers to consider in designing our military forces and our arms control policies.

Despite their importance to our future, Soviet leaders remain a mystery to most Americans. They are, writes *New York Times* reporter Steven Roberts, "a set of shadowy figures over in the corner that everybody is talking about and trying to understand." Because the Soviet Union is a closed society compared with the United States, public understanding of Soviet leadership attitudes has been hampered by a dearth of information. The informed judgments of experts on the Soviet Union do, however, offer a starting point for greater public understanding of the issues that divide or unite the nuclear superpowers.

■ Soviet Nuclear Doctrine

The destruction of a Korean airliner by a Soviet fighter plane in September 1983 shocked and sobered the international community. The tragic incident demonstrated the kind of miscalculations, tensions, and apparent irrationality that could spark a nuclear war in the future. It also evoked understandable public hostility toward the Soviet Union and raised serious questions about the values and attitudes of Soviet leaders.

Analysis of Soviet nuclear doctrine is a speculative and subjective exercise. Nonetheless, evidence of how Soviet leaders think about nuclear war can be gleaned from an examination of their public positions on three basic issues: Could nuclear war be survived and won? Could nuclear war be limited? Should nuclear weapons be used to strike first?

Survival or Suicide: The Soviet View

At the heart of American fears is a basic concern that nuclear war may be more "thinkable" to Soviet leaders than it is to us. A 1977 article in *Commentary* magazine drew attention to this issue with its controversial title, "Why the Soviet Union Thinks It Could Fight and Win a Nuclear War." Author Richard Pipes, a Harvard professor and formerly a top advisor on President Reagan's National Security Council staff, examined officers' training manuals and military journals for evidence of Soviet thinking. Upon reviewing these documents, he concluded that nuclear war is not considered suicidal by Soviet leaders; rather, he claimed, their military preparations reflect Soviet intentions to emerge from nuclear war as a viable and victorious society.

Pipes' conclusions have sparked criticism from many individuals, among them defense journalist Fred Kaplan and Soviet emigré and scholar Dimitri Simes. They maintain that Soviet or even American military literature is helpful only insofar as it reflects *military science*—that is, operational plans for warfare in the event of hostilities. Accordingly, Soviet military journals, like U.S. defense manuals, can offer insight into how a nation might operate its nuclear arsenal should deterrence fail. Such plans should not, they say, be equated with *strategic doctrine*—those beliefs and values that shape official policy on the use of nuclear weapons.

Since the 1950s, official statements by Soviet leaders consistently have acknowledged the unparalleled destructiveness of nuclear weapons:

> The consequences of atomic-hydrogen bomb war would persist during the lives of many generations and would result in disease, death, and would cripple the human race.
>
> Nikita Khrushchev, 1963

> It is a dangerous madness to try to defeat each other in the arms race and to count on victory in a nuclear war. I shall add that only he who has decided to commit suicide can start a nuclear war in the hope of emerging a victor from it.
>
> Leonid Brezhnev, 1981

> Mankind cannot endlessly put up with the arms race and with wars unless it wants to put its future at stake.
>
> Yuri Andropov, 1982

Such pronouncements are dismissed by some Westerners as mere propaganda, masking a Soviet view that nuclear war is survivable. Fritz Ermarth, Pipes' predecessor in the Carter Administration, explains this interpretation in his 1978 article on Soviet strategic thought:

> ... the [Soviet] system decided it *had* to believe in survival and victory of some form. Not to believe so would mean that the most basic processes of history,

on which Soviet ideology and political legitimacy are founded, could be derailed by the technological works of man and the caprice of a historically doomed opponent.

This perspective often is reinforced by reference to the Soviet civil defense program, a plan that envisions large-scale evacuation and sheltering of Soviet citizens. Such preparations are construed to demonstrate Soviet confidence in limiting post-war damage in their society.

On the other hand, questions surrounding the viability of civil defense are common knowledge to American and Soviet leaders. In a 1978 study, the U.S. Central Intelligence Agency concluded:

> The [Soviets] cannot have confidence . . . in the degree of protection their civil defense would afford them, given the many uncertainties . . . . We do not believe that the Soviets' present civil defenses would embolden them deliberately to expose the U.S.S.R. to a higher level of nuclear attack.

Limited Nuclear War: The Soviet View

Despite efforts to contain territorial damage, Soviet leaders express little confidence in escalation control—limiting nuclear war short of full-scale hostilities, once it has begun. This perspective can be traced to many factors, including the geographic proximity of the Soviet Union to potential "hot spots" (such as the European theater) as well as the deterrent effect of such a stance on U.S. military planning. Raymond Garthoff, former SALT negotiator and U.S. Ambassador to Bulgaria, offers his interpretation of why Soviet leaders give little credence to limited war theories:

> One purpose for saying this, of course, is to dissuade us from any belief that we would have limited nuclear options, such as in a war that began as a conventional conflict, whether in Europe, in the Middle East, or in any other situation that was going against us. But they also have a genuine concern that any limited nuclear warfare . . . would carry very great risks of escalating out of control, and therefore should be avoided and not pursued as a strategy by either side.

That such a position appears to be in the Soviet interest is not surprising, given the danger posed by all-out nuclear confrontation. In the words of Maxwell Taylor, former Chairman of the Joint Chiefs of Staff, the United States has the potential to "inflict on the Soviets damage and losses in a few hours at least equivalent to those they suffered in four years of World War II," when 20 million Russian citizens died.

Striking First: The Soviet View

The legacy of World War II—and Germany's surprise attack on Russia—shaped the direction of Soviet military strategy during the 1950s. As a result of their experience, Soviet military planners became wedded to the policy of preemption: if the Soviet Union believed that enemy attack was imminent, it should strike first to neutralize enemy forces.

Today, the fear of a first strike is a driving factor in both U.S. and Soviet nuclear strategy. According to some Western observers, the acquisition of powerful counterforce weapons by the Soviet Union is strong evidence of its first-strike intentions. This interpretation is challenged by other observers who question whether Soviet leaders, despite their military capability against American land-based missiles, would be confident of their success under actual attack conditions. As Western defense scholar David Holloway writes in *The Soviet Union and the Arms Race,* "There is little evidence in Soviet thinking of the kind of technological hubris that would be required to launch such a horrendously risky strike."

Some observers suggest, on the other hand, that the Soviet Union is at least as concerned as the United States about being the target of a first-strike attack. Because the Soviets have 73 percent of their nuclear warheads on land-based ICBMs (compared to 22 percent of U.S. nuclear warheads), American ICBMs theoretically could destroy a larger percentage of Soviet strategic forces than vice versa.

This perceived vulnerability has led Soviet leaders to consider several options for launching their nuclear weapons. They reportedly are prepared to launch under attack and may even opt to launch on warning, a practice that would place the Soviet nuclear arsenal on a hair trigger in a crisis. Such preparations may evidence a Soviet readiness to strike the first blow *if* a nuclear attack against Soviet forces seemed imminent. They do not necessarily imply, however, that Soviet leaders would be more willing than their American counterparts to initiate the use of nuclear arms. As former U.S. Ambassador to Moscow Averell Harriman asserts:

> I am certain that Soviet leaders are as concerned to avoid a nuclear war as we are. I have seen how the Second World War scarred not only a generation but the very soul of every Soviet citizen—even those born a decade after the guns fell silent. They have no desire to repeat that experience.

In this context, arms control may provide an opportunity for the Soviet Union to serve its interest in avoiding nuclear war. "They're serious about it," explains chief SALT II negotiator Paul Warnke, "because they recognize that their national

CommonConcern: Non-Proliferation

Curbing the spread of nuclear weapons "is one of the rare instances in which both the Americans and the Russians seem to be fully aware that their interests are exactly parallel," writes physicist Herbert York, the first Director of Defense Research and Engineering for the federal government. Both nations recognize, at least in principle, that as the number of countries with nuclear weapons increases, so does the likelihood of nuclear war.

To address this problem, the United States, the Soviet Union, and Great Britain, along with 59 other nations, signed the Non-Proliferation Treaty (NPT) on July 11, 1968. (There are now over 100 signatories.) Under the treaty's terms, non-nuclear nations (the "have nots") agreed to forgo developing their own nuclear weapons in the future in exchange for three promises from nations that already had them (the "haves").

First, nuclear nations pledged to help the "have nots" acquire nuclear technology for peaceful application in domestic power programs. At the same time, *all* signatories agreed to subject their nuclear facilities and shipments to supervision by the United Nations-sponsored International Atomic Energy Agency.

Second, the "haves" pledged to refrain from helping any other nation obtain nuclear weapons.

Third, the nuclear nations pledged to undertake serious negotiations to end the nu-

survival is at stake." In a similar vein, *Time* diplomatic correspondent Strobe Talbott writes, "My own conviction is that they are genuinely worried about the increased danger of war that would accompany an all-out, no-holds-barred escalation in the military rivalry between us."

Many Americans, however, understandably are skeptical of "trusting the Russians" and question whether Soviet leaders are seriously committed to negotiating treaties. In examining this question, it is important to consider both the Soviets' incentives to negotiate and their behavior during past arms control negotiations.

■ Soviet Interests in Arms Control

Apart from serving a mutual interest in nuclear peace, arms control has the potential to further distinctly Soviet interests in several specific ways.

First, arms control agreements can codify the "strategic equilibrium" between the United States and Soviet Union that is highly prized by Soviet leaders. As Talbott explains:

> Over the past 15 or 20 years, they have been trying harder, like Avis. In terms of nuclear strength, they've established themselves as our co-equals, although they still lag behind us in many other respects, of course. And they see arms control as a way of certifying that equality which they believe they've achieved.

Moreover, negotiated arrangements can restrain U.S. innovations in weaponry, such as cruise missile technology, that represent to the Soviets an American advantage over them.

Second, the arms control process can advance the political interests of the Soviet Union by reinforcing its status as a nuclear superpower, set apart and secure from less-armed nations. For example, a Soviet precondition for beginning SALT was the completion of the Non-proliferation Treaty to settle the nuclear future of Germany. Furthermore, Soviet participation in arms control talks can be exploited for propaganda purposes and enhance the nation's desired image as a country committed to regional and global security.

Finally, Soviet leaders, like American leaders, seem to be acutely aware of the financial burden of the arms race. From the Soviet viewpoint, the U.S. military buildup poses an economic as well as military threat, one designed to bankrupt the Soviet economy by forcing its leaders to match U.S. investments in weaponry. In this context, arms control offers Soviet leaders a way to curb weapons competition, particularly at a time when the Soviet economy is performing poorly. Malcolm Toon, a former U.S. Ambassador to Moscow, offers this assessment of Soviet interests:

They do recognize that the arms race imposes a painful burden on their economy, and they would much rather turn it down somewhat by negotiating an arms control agreement with us as they did in SALT II. But this interest does not reflect an inherent weakness in their economy that we can take advantage of.

The best assumption we can make is that they will do whatever they feel is necessary and make their people pay whatever price.

To say that arms control furthers Soviet interests is not to suggest that nuclear negotiations are a "no-win" situation for the United States. The incentive for both superpowers to reach agreement is the prospect that mutual self-interest—and mutual survival—will be served. Indeed, successful arms control between the United States and the Soviet Union depends on this mutually beneficial framework. As foreign service officer Robert Einhorn observes in his article, "Treaty Compliance,"

> If they both believe their national interests can be served by negotiating and adhering to arms control agreements, they will have the incentive to adopt . . . pragmatic and constructive approaches . . . .

■ Soviet Negotiating Record

In a recent report for the Carnegie Endowment for International Peace, a panel of strategic experts examined specific areas of past nuclear arms negotiations that highlight, in their words, "general aspects of the Soviet approach to arms control." The main findings of this panel are summarized below.

Soviet Flexibility: ABM Limits

The deployment of a Soviet anti-missile defense system in 1964 led the United States to call for negotiations to limit ABM weaponry—a proposal that was initially rejected by the Soviet Union. Subsequent American interest in deploying a U.S. ABM system, coupled with a close but favorable Congressional vote on the issue, led the Soviets to change their earlier bargaining position and seek restrictions on ABM deployment. This experience, writes the Carnegie Panel, highlights "the ability of the U.S.S.R. to deal flexibly with some issues" and to shift their negotiating approach "in light of prevailing political and strategic realities."

Soviet Intransigence: ICBM Limits

During SALT I, SALT II and START, the Soviet Union consistently has opposed American efforts to place selective lim-

clear arms race and eventually eliminate their own nuclear arsenals.

In 1985, the NPT, in accord with its provisions, is scheduled for a third review conference aimed at assessing progress toward realizing the treaty's goals. Although the number of nuclear states has remained at five since 1964*, one new country—India—has tested a nuclear device, ten additional countries are believed capable of building a nuclear bomb, eleven could have the bomb in six years, and four more could have the bomb within ten years, according to a *Newsweek* report on December 5, 1983.

These developments may be attributed to many factors, including the political and military motivations of "threshold states," the competition among exporters of nuclear technology, the refusal of nonparties to accept the safeguards established by the NPT, and the inability of the superpowers to demonstrate "good faith" efforts toward disarmament.

In this latter context, many arms control specialists view the successful completion of a Comprehensive Test Ban Treaty as an essential step toward preventing the emergence of new nuclear nations. Such an agreement, writes Senator Charles McC. Mathias, Jr. (R-MD), would serve both "common sense and our common humanity . . . [by] proscribing future dangerous nuclear testing by the United States and the Soviet Union— and providing an example for the rest of the world to follow." ●

*These are the United States, the Soviet Union, Great Britain, France, and China. Neither France nor China has signed the NPT.

"You Say 'Tomato'..."

The challenge of reconciling U.S. and Soviet views toward arms control is highlighted by the simple yet controversial term "strategic." From the American standpoint, strategic weapons are long-range forces that can be launched from the homeland of one superpower, or its submarines at sea, against the homeland of the other. To the Soviet Union, however, any weapon that can strike the motherland is a strategic weapon, whether launched from American or European soil. This fundamental disagreement is complicating efforts to limit strategic and intermediate-range nuclear forces under the aegis of separate START and INF negotiations. The inextricable relationship between these talks—for example, long-range Soviet missiles aimed at the United States can be readily retargeted against Europe—has led a number of observers to call for merging the two negotiations in a more compatible and practical framework for agreement. •

its on modern land-based missiles, the core feature of the Soviet nuclear arsenal. Although some negotiated restraints, such as SALT II's MIRV ceiling, have the practical effect of limiting the size of this force, Soviet leaders have granted few concessions on the ICBM issue. This pattern of behavior, writes the Carnegie Panel, suggests that "basic [Soviet] strategic positions are not open to major change, except incrementally over an extended period."

Soviet Compromise: Cruise Missile Limits

In the early stages of SALT I, when neither superpower had deployed long-range cruise missiles, the United States proposed a complete ban on such weaponry; however, discussion on this matter was set aside for the conclusion of the Interim Agreement. Subsequent posturing by both nations—to protect select aspects of their own cruise missile forces while banning those deemed threatening—led to a compromise under SALT II that placed temporary limits on ground- and sea-launched cruise missile deployments. This record exemplifies a "mixed outcome," notes the Carnegie Panel, in which Soviet preferences both failed and prevailed. Furthermore, "it points up that the Soviet Union, as well as the United States, has been slow to grasp the implications of advances in technologies . . . ."

In sum, an appreciation of the Soviet stake in nuclear negotiations and an awareness of Soviet bargaining patterns in the past can help us appraise the prospects for future agreement. While the obstacles are large, there is cause for optimism. As McGeorge Bundy, Special Assistant for National Security Affairs to Presidents Kennedy and Johnson, points out in an article entitled "What If the Charges Are True?":

> The most dangerous moment we have had with them, the Cuban missile crisis, was caused by terrible failures of perception on both sides, and its peaceful resolution was the consequence not only of determination and strength, but of intense communication. Arms-control negotiations have a much more complex history, but the common testimony of American negotiators of all persuasions is that when we are serious, the Soviets can be, too.

Such advice is particularly compelling in this period of strained superpower relations when arms control is both more important and more difficult to achieve. The lack of progress in recent negotiations, capped by the Soviet walkout in Geneva, has sharpened public debate over U.S.-Soviet relations in general.

■ Soviet-American Relations

After 50 years of formal diplomatic relations between the United States and the Soviet Union, many Western observers are alarmed by the level of distrust that pervades current dealings between the two governments. Writing in September 1983, William Hyland, former Deputy Assistant for National Security in the Ford Administration, offered this assessment:

> Superpower relations are bad. There is no political dialogue, little trade, no bilateral cooperation, no cultural exchange and, now, not even occasional diplomatic contact at higher levels. The entire relationship seems to be reduced to two shaky arms control negotiations in Geneva and the sale of grain.

With the recent derailment of the INF and START negotiations—and the mutual build-up of medium-range missiles in the European theater—many fear that the United States and the Soviet Union are on a political and military collision course. As former U.S. Ambassador to the Soviet Union Thomas Watson, Jr. observed in November 1983:

> There are signs of growing crisis in the air . . . . [T]here is a hair-trigger situation in the Middle East and a potential crisis over the oil shipping lanes out of the Persian Gulf. Either could lead to superpower confrontation. American and Soviet leaders have traded vitriolic attacks. Negotiations in Geneva on medium-range missiles are indefinitely suspended, and there have been no meaningful discussions on heading off crises in which these weapons might be used. In short, at no time has our existence been threatened as it is today.

This grim picture is sobering for many Americans whose recent memory recalls the more hopeful "decade of détente"—a period in the 1970s when East-West diplomacy benefited by increased trade, contact, and cooperation. Subsequent events—in particular the Soviet invasion of Afghanistan, the imposition of martial law in Poland, and the destruction of a Korean airliner by a Soviet warplane—have created deep strains in superpower relations and heightened public mistrust of Soviet leaders.

Few Americans would challenge the proposition that improving U.S.-Soviet relations could reduce the risk of nuclear war, but people disagree regarding the confidence they have in diplomatic efforts with the Soviet Union. As John Steinbruner of the Brookings Institution summarizes the problem:

> Are we capable of serious statesmanship in dealing with an opponent that many of us hate, most of us fear, and none of us trust?

The Question of Linkage

A recurrent theme in the arms control debate is the question of *linkage:* Should American participation in agreements with the Soviet Union be tied to Soviet behavior in other military and non-military arenas? Advocates of this approach maintain that arms control negotiations cannot and should not be "insulated" from U.S.-Soviet relations. Moreover, they suggest that linkage provides the United States with important political leverage in the diplomatic arena as well as at the bargaining table.

Other observers challenge the strategy of rewarding or punishing Soviet actions via the arms control process. Cyrus Vance, Secretary of State in the Carter Administration, and former National Security Council staff member Robert Hunter write:

> . . . we must not encumber arms control negotiations with artificial ties to other issues that are in dispute between the East and West. In fact, arms control agreements are either in our national security interest and should be pursued on their own merits or they are not in our national interest and should not be pursued, however positive the diplomatic climate with the Soviet Union. In short, linkage is a critical mistake . . . .

Chief SALT I negotiator Gerard Smith writes in a similar vein:

Today, the challenge of preventing nuclear war requires Americans to reappraise relations with our principal world rival. During the past few years, dealings between the United States and the Soviet Union have been confined largely to arms competition and, until recently, arms negotiation—both of which reflect a preoccupation with military issues. In this period of strained relations, some observers question the effectiveness of this approach in preserving peace and its value in serving American interests. Writing in the summer of 1983, Senator Charles McC. Mathias, Jr. (R-MD) explained:

> In a poisoned political atmosphere we have narrowed what might be an extensive range of contacts to a set of limited negotiations more likely to stimulate paranoia and propaganda than progress . . . . And by addressing a militaristic society only on the strongest ground it occupies, we limit the influence we can have, the alternatives we can pursue.

Alternative avenues of superpower contact include a range of activities that were tried experimentally during the period of détente and offer a blueprint for cooperation in the future. For example, there are 75 U.S.-Soviet bilateral agreements at present on environmental cooperation, health, housing, agriculture and energy, maritime affairs, trade, commerce and aviation. In addition, over 500 U.S. corporations have signed agreements with the Soviet Union for commodity sales and scientific and technological exchanges of non-strategic goods. During recent years, writes Carl Marcy of the American Committee on East-West Accord, these agreements have fallen into disarray but could be resurrected as part of a new diplomatic strategy that includes efforts to expand trade and widen economic cooperation.

In addition, the idea of annual summit meetings between U.S. and Soviet leaders is receiving considerable attention among diplomacy experts. A regular summit between senior figures has the potential to serve several valuable goals. The annual deadline provides an action-forcing mechanism, encouraging both countries' officials to narrow their differences so that agreement can be reached. The prospect of a summit also may inhibit adventurous or provocative behavior beforehand. Most important, face-to-face meetings of national leaders can enhance mutual understanding and help reduce the risk of miscalculation in a crisis.

Such initiatives may be plausible in the long run and lay the foundation for a more well-rounded relationship between the United States and the Soviet Union. In the short run, however, neither nation is likely to welcome highly-publicized overtures, given the deep-seated feelings of hostility on both sides. Instead, cautions former U.S. Ambassador to the Soviet Union George Kennan, a program of quiet diplomacy is better suited to the current environment. As he explains in his article "Inching Away from the Danger Zone:"

> There can be no room here for angry polemics and the many recriminations over things past that have marked recent exchanges . . . . It means meeting the Soviet side at normal levels of communication, avoiding discussions over motivation, sticking strictly to the practical business at hand, and seeing whether useful smaller areas of agreement cannot be found, even where the great ones are lacking.

Seizing even limited opportunities for diplomacy will require a dramatic shift in the agenda of the superpowers and in the attitudes of their leaders. "Mistrust has to be tackled," writes historian Barbara Tuchman, "and that is the hardest task." Nonetheless, national security—indeed national survival—demands that *every* effort be made to reverse the current dangerous trend in U.S.-Soviet relations. As long ago as 1957, General Omar Bradley saw the virtue of this path when he wrote:

> It may be that the problems of accommodation in a world split by rival ideologies are more difficult than those with which we have struggled in the construction of ballistic missiles. But I believe that if we apply to these human problems the energy, creativity and perseverance we have devoted to science, even problems of accommodation will yield to reason.

. . . a useful arms control agreement should not be made conditional or "linked" to progress in other areas. Such a "linkage" concept may find support in history but in this nuclear age, when rival nations live under the threat of almost instant destruction, a chance to reduce that threat has independent value. Adversary nations should grasp any such opportunity even though their other relations are not improving.

Smith's message—that arms control should proceed even, or especially, in the face of international tension—is not meant to suggest that treaties alone can prevent nuclear war. Rather, it reaffirms the importance of pursuing *all* forms of diplomacy—including diplomatic agreements—to reduce the likelihood of superpower conflict. •

■ Selected Sources

James H. Billington, "A Time of Danger, An Opening for Dialogue," *The Washington Post,* November 20, 1983.

McGeorge Bundy, "What If the Charges Are True?" *The Washington Post,* January 9, 1983.

Carnegie Panel on U.S. Security and the Future of Arms Control, *Challenges for U.S. National Security* (Carnegie Endowment for International Peace, 1983).

Noel Gayler, "How to Break the Momentum of the Nuclear Arms Race," *The New York Times Magazine,* April 25, 1982.

Michael R. Gordon, "Rubles for Defense—Are the Soviets Really Outspending the Pentagon?" *National Journal,* April 11, 1981.

Sanford Gottlieb, *What About the Russians?* (Student/Teacher Organization to Prevent Nuclear War, 1982).

Ground Zero, *What About the Russians—and Nuclear War?* (Ground Zero Fund, Inc., 1983).

W. Averell Harriman, "Let's Negotiate with Andropov," *The New York Times,* January 2, 1983.

David Holloway, *The Soviet Union and the Arms Race* (Yale University Press, 1983).

William G. Hyland, "Eventually, We Will Have to Return to Diplomacy," *The Washington Post,* September 25, 1983.

Fred Kaplan, "Russian and American Intentions," *The Atlantic Monthly,* July 1982.

George F. Kennan, *The Nuclear Delusion: Soviet-American Relations in the Atomic Age* (Pantheon Books, 1982).

———, "Inching Away from the Danger Zone," *The Washington Post,* October 11, 1983.

Benjamin S. Lambeth, "What Deters? An Assessment of the Soviet View," and Fritz W. Ermarth, "Contrasts in American and Soviet Strategic Thought," in *American Defense Policy,* edited by John F. Reichart and Steven R. Sturm (Johns Hopkins University Press, 1982).

Charles McC. Mathias, Jr., "Habitual Hatred—Unsound Policy," *Foreign Affairs,* Summer 1983.

Carl Marcy, "U.S.-Soviet Relations," *The Bulletin of Atomic Scientists,* October 1982.

Alan F. Neidle, ed., *Nuclear Negotiations: Reassessing Arms Control Goals in U.S.-Soviet Relations* (The University of Texas at Austin, 1982).

Richard Pipes, "Why the Soviet Union Thinks It Could Fight and Win a Nuclear War," *Commentary,* July 1977.

Steven V. Roberts, "Gambling on the Russian Response to MX Missile," *The New York Times,* June 4, 1983.

Senate Committee on Foreign Relations, *The United States*

and the Soviet Union: Prospects for the Relationship (U.S. Government Printing Office, 1983.)

Barbara Tuchman, "The Alternative to Arms Control," *The New York Times Magazine,* April 18, 1982.

Thomas J. Watson, Jr., "Establish A Security Panel," *The New York Times,* November 29, 1983.

V. CAN CITIZENS MAKE A DIFFERENCE?

In no other area today is it more important for the principle of public control over public officials to be exercised.

Admiral Stansfield Turner, Retired
Former Director, Central Intelligence Agency
1982

How Can Citizens Influence Nuclear Arms Policy?

One of the most striking aspects of nuclear arms policy is the sheer complexity of the subject. Learning the basic issues—from military strategy to U.S.-Soviet relations—can cause one to feel *more,* rather than less, intimidated by the problem of preventing nuclear war.

Nonetheless, it is not the magnitude of the problem that poses the greatest obstacle to its solution. Rather it is, as General Omar Bradley warned in 1957, our "colossal indifference" to it.

For more than three decades, most American citizens have avoided the debate over nuclear arms policy. We have watched nuclear weapons grow more numerous and more deadly over time, we have seen the superpowers come perilously close to confrontation, we have witnessed the hands of the "doomsday clock" move closer to midnight.* Yet we have remained comfortably on the sidelines, leaving the management of the arms race to a closed circle of government officials, military planners, and scientists.

At last, however, a truly national debate on nuclear arms policy has begun. The topic comes up at the dinner table, on the TV screen, and in just about every magazine and newspaper that passes hands. Today, more citizens than ever before are discussing the threat of nuclear war.

Despite the signs of public interest, some commentators view this new-found citizen voice with caution. Writing in the summer of 1982, the editors of *The New York Times* questioned whether citizens are prepared to go "beyond anxiety" and help frame policies to reduce the threat of nuclear war. It is a question we must ask and answer ourselves.

It is easy enough to appreciate the dangers of nuclear war. One has only to read of the effects of nuclear weapons or the testimony of Hiroshima survivors to understand the stakes involved.

It is even easy, relatively speaking, to understand the issues that shape the policy debate. A wealth of material on arms

---

*The "doomsday clock" appears monthly on the cover of *The Bulletin of the Atomic Scientists.* The location of the minute hand symbolizes the immediacy of the threat of nuclear disaster. At the close of 1983, the clock's hand was moved to 3 minutes to midnight.

control, nuclear strategy, and the military balance—to name a few topics—is now available from libraries, government agencies, public interest organizations, and other sources.

It is harder—at least at first blush—to *join* the policy debate and to influence its outcome. We ask ourselves whether one individual can make a difference and, if so, where to begin. Obstacles to public participation in the nuclear debate surely abound. The complex nature of nuclear arms policy—involving, as it does, sensitive questions of national security—confers on the military establishment a seemingly exclusive right to chart its course.

Today, however, more and more individuals recognize the limits of military might in the nuclear age and appreciate the need for political and diplomatic approaches to the problem of preventing nuclear war. As political scientist Seweryn Bialer observes, "The key to American and Soviet security lies not with weapon makers but with political leaders—in their willingness and ability to lower the overheated temperature of Soviet-American confrontation."

Ultimately, then, individual citizens have a role to play in the nuclear arms debate, not as outside intruders in some forbidden province, but as rightful participants in the American political process. It is in this capacity that citizens are empowered to help our elected leaders shape national policies on nuclear arms and arms control.

According to some observers, the lack of a comparable role for Soviet citizens skews the balance unfairly, creating a sort of "peace gap" between the United States and the Soviet Union. To be sure, the Soviet premier is not besieged with letters from outraged citizens demanding that he restrain their nation's nuclear weapons program; no human chains surround Soviet military bases.

But while it is true that Soviet citizens cannot make their views known in the same manner as American citizens, it is also true that Soviet leaders have strong reasons to participate in serious negotiations to limit nuclear arms. The Soviet economy can ill afford too much defense spending. More important, Soviet leaders recognize that virtually every nuclear weapon not in the Soviet Union is aimed at it.

It is also clear that someone has to lead the way. With so much at stake, we simply cannot stand by idly while the arms race continues unabated. At the end of the Second World War, the United States helped rebuild Europe through the Marshall Plan. In a similar spirit, through serious negotiations, the United States can now lead the world to reduce the threat of nuclear war. But it will not do so unless its citizens command it to lead the way.

The power of citizen action is borne out by the history of arms control since World War II. "[O]n only two occasions have limits on U.S. and Soviet forces that were significant or perceived to be significant been achieved," observes Lawrence Weiler, former Counselor to the U.S. Arms Control and Disarmament Agency, "and those were the two times when the public got involved." He explains:

> The two agreements were the Limited Test Ban and the ABM Treaty. The Test Ban was achieved because the women of America got concerned about radioactive fallout . . . . The ABM debate of 1970 produced a climate which made it clear to officials that there would not be public support for continuing with the Safeguard ABM program if a viable alternative, the ABM Treaty, were possible. The reason that these are the only two instances of significant arms control is because the momentum of the arms race and the strength of forces propelling it forward are too great to be stopped without public involvement and pressure.

Indeed, history also has shown that the *absence* of public involvement can affect the prospects for arms control. Citizen pressure four years ago could have made a difference in the debate over SALT II. Instead, citizen apathy allowed the U.S. Senate to defer consideration of the much-needed SALT II Treaty, which remains unratified today.

How, then, can citizens influence the outcome of current debate on preventing nuclear war?

The prerequisite for informed political debate is a concerned citizenry that continually asks questions. Do we need this proposed weapons program? Does this nuclear arms policy promote the common good? Is sufficient progress being made in arms control negotiations? Such constructive oversight provides a useful prod to national leaders responsible for national security—the president who fashions our foreign policy program and ultimately commands our military forces; the members of Congress who oversee the defense budget process and advise the president on arms control policy. By holding these officials accountable for their positions on nuclear arms and arms control, "it reminds them that they have to earn support. It isn't theirs simply by right of place," observes columnist Flora Lewis.

The tools available for political action are plentiful. Each of us can find the means most comfortable to us as individuals to participate in the national dialogue on nuclear arms policy. We can express our opinions—and raise our questions—in letters and telephone calls to elected officials, letters to editors of newspapers and magazines, comments on radio call-in shows, and discussions at public forums on nuclear arms policy.

There are, moreover, a number of national organizations for individuals to join as a focal point for their activity. These organizations—Common Cause is one—bring the collective weight of their memberships to bear on political leaders in Washington to persuade them, quite simply, that the arms race must end.

Neighborhood groups, religious groups, professional associations, even a collection of friends can accomplish much by working together, particularly during an election year. They can poll candidates for office regarding their views on nuclear arms policy and publicize candidates' positions among the electorate. Indeed, every citizen has in hand one of the most effective weapons for political change: the vote.

Citizens also can help by volunteering their time and effort to aid candidates who are committed to nuclear arms control. During a 1982 interview, Representative Edward Markey (D-MA), a sponsor of the nuclear freeze resolution, told *The New York Times:*

> Everyone in the House that I've spoken to recently who has talked to their constituents about the nuclear arms issue ends up walking out of the room with 15 or 20 more volunteers for their campaign next fall.

Citizen action—whatever its form—thus can send a valuable message to our elected officials. In the spring of 1983, for example, the House of Representatives approved a resolution favoring a bilateral nuclear weapons freeze. The initiative passed in large part because so many towns, cities, counties and states passed resolutions of their own favoring the freeze. Those resolutions got on the ballot because enough individuals signed petitions to get them there.

Ultimately, it is the sustained, concerted action of individuals that will commit our political leaders to navigate and negotiate a new path to security. We otherwise will remain imperiled not only by the existence of nuclear weapons but the persistence of apathy in the nuclear age. The challenge of preventing nuclear war demands our participation, imagination, and whole-hearted determination as a people.

INDEX

*The following entries direct the reader to the pages containing the **definition** and **main discussion** of key terms.*

This book was set in 10 point ITC Garamond by Creative Communications Corporation. It was printed on 60# Williamsburg paper with 10 point Warrenflo Cover stock by District Creative Printing.

The book was designed by Tim Kenney and produced by Betsy Woldman. Illustrations were by James Yang.

BASIC TRAINING

Announcing two new Common Cause books on defense and arms control that: cut through the jargon; summarize facts and figures and lay out the issue; provide a not-for-experts-only reference tool for educators, activists and others who want answers and straight talk on defense-related issues.

Written in readable, down to earth prose, these are books that at last give activists and concerned citizens alike the information they need to participate in the ongoing debate over national security policy.

Up In Arms tackles the hard questions: How grave is the threat of nuclear war? What is the nuclear balance of forces? How should we deal with the Russians? How can citizens help prevent nuclear war?

Defense Dollars and Sense demystifies the defense budget process, revealing: how pork barrel politics is big business for Congress and bad policy for citizens; how bureaucratic politics leads to spending billions for weapons we don't need; why no one seems to know why we need some of our expensive weapons.

In an era of increased defense spending and concern about international security, citizens can no longer afford to leave defense policy up to the "experts." Here are the books that answer the questions more and more citizens are asking.

New!
From Common Cause
books to inform and
empower citizens.

"... provides an essential demystification of the defense budget—how it is made, what it contains and how it can be controlled. Real national security planning requires [such] popular understanding."
—Gordon Adams
Director
Defense Budget Project

"...very helpful reading for a citizen who is concerned [about] nuclear weapons, nuclear doctrine and nuclear arms control, particularly if he or she wants to do something about them."
—Lawrence Weiler
former Counselor of the U.S. Arms Control Agency and member of the U.S. SALT I delegation.

FREE COPY!

YES, I want to be informed. I understand you will send me free with each order a copy of **You Can Prevent Nuclear War** and you will pay all postage and handling charges.
Please send me:

QUANTITY

☐ **Up In Arms** at $3.50 _____
☐ **Defense Dollars
And Sense** at $4.50 _____

*Common Cause members
deduct $1.00 from each book.*

Total Enclosed _____

☐ Sign me up, at no charge, for the Common Cause Nuclear Arms Alert Network, joining 50,000 citizens to act quickly and effectively when there is a need to lobby Congress or the White House. Also, start my free subscription to *Hotline,* a newsletter which will keep me up-to-date on the nuclear arms debate.

NAME _____

ADDRESS _____

CITY _____ STATE _____ ZIP _____

Please make check payable to Common Cause and send with this order to:
**Common Cause Guides
2030 M Street, NW
Washington, D.C. 20036
Attention: Issue Mail, Box 66**

Bookstore and bulk order inquiries are welcome.